Sunset
Mexican
COOK BOOK

BY THE EDITORS OF SUNSET BOOKS
AND SUNSET MAGAZINE

SUNSET PUBLISHING CORPORATION • MENLO PARK, CALIFORNIA

Research & Text
Tori Bunting

Contributing Editor
Susan Warton

Coordinating Editor
Cornelia Fogle

Design
Cynthia Hanson

Illustrations
H. Tom Kamifuji

Photographers

Glenn Christiansen: *126.* **Tom Wyatt:** *27,
43, 62, 70, 78, 86, 94.* **Nikolay Zurek:** *3, 6,
11, 14, 19, 22, 30, 35, 38, 46, 51, 54, 59, 67,
75, 83, 91, 99, 102, 107, 110, 115, 118, 123.*

Photo Stylists

Susan Massey-Weil: *38.* **JoAnn Masaoka
Van Atta:** *3, 6, 11, 14, 19, 22, 27, 30, 35, 43,
46, 51, 54, 59, 62, 67, 70, 75, 78, 83, 86, 91,
94, 99, 102, 107, 110, 115, 118, 123.*

Cover: *Sample Mexico's spirited flavors with
Carnitas Fiesta (recipe on page 37). Flour
tortillas enfolding tender pork and beans
are adorned with three lively salsas and a
sprinkling of crumbled fresh Mexican cheese.
Design by Susan Bryant. Photography by
Nikolay Zurek. Photo styling by Susan
Massey-Weil. Food styling by Tori Bunting.*

Editor, Sunset Books: Elizabeth L. Hogan

Third printing January 1991

A Taste of Mexico

Import the vibrant flavors of Mexican cooking right into your own kitchen using this book as your guide. For every kind of meal, you'll discover unique recipes full of south-of-the-border color and flavor. Let them add adventure to family meals as well as special occasions.

Whether you're looking for a foolproof enchilada or a no-fail flan, a spicy seafood stew or a light, yet zesty, salad, you'll find a marvelous selection here. Learn the basics for making ever-popular Mexican tortillas, tacos, burritos, tamales, and more in the special chapter called Mexican Favorites. Then explore the complete world of Mexican cooking, from appetizers to desserts, in the remaining chapters and special features.

You won't have to sacrifice convenience as you bring the authentic flavors of Mexico into your kitchen. Finding Mexican ingredients means only a quick trip to a well-stocked supermarket; many north-of-the-border cities also boast Hispanic markets. A guide to chiles, the heart and soul of Mexican food, and other specialty ingredients is included here for your information.

For their skillful and careful editing of the manuscript, we thank Fran Feldman and Stacey Pollard. A special thanks goes to L. Alberto Mier, of La Canasta in San Francisco, for his helpful advice and consultation on Spanish terminology. We also thank The Best of All Worlds, Cottonwood, Crate & Barrel, and Sibila Savage for their generosity in sharing props for use in our photographs.

For our recipes, we provide a nutritional analysis (see page 5) prepared by Hill Nutrition Associates, Inc., of New York.

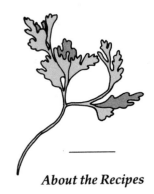

About the Recipes

All of the recipes in this book were tested and developed in the *Sunset* test kitchens.

*Food and Entertaining Editor
Sunset Magazine*
Jerry Anne Di Vecchio

Rustic molcajetes (stone mortars and pestle) authentically present colorful and flavorful Tomatilla Salsa (left), Salsa Fresca (center), and Smoky Roasted Salsa (right). Recipes on pages 48 and 49.

Contents

A Cook's Tour of Mexico

BAJA CALIFORNIA

⊙Chihuahua

⊙Monterrey

⊙Mazatlan

Tampico ⊙

⊙Merida

⊙Guadalajara

⊙Mexico City
Puebla ⊙ ⊙Veracruz

YUCATAN PENINSULA

⊙Oaxaca

Mexico

Mexican food, like Mexico itself, is a vibrant blend of colors, textures, flavors, and fragments of history. One of the most ancient cuisines of the Western world, it's also one that adapts easily to the contemporary kitchen, for both everyday cooking and festive entertaining.

Though more famous north of the border for such popular dishes as tacos and enchiladas, Mexican cuisine also offers an enticing array of roasted meats and game, succulent seafood, fresh vegetables and fruits, and delicate pastries and desserts. Distinguishing each region of the country is an outstanding local cuisine, offering specialties to delight and surprise every palate.

The recipes in this book have been chosen to bring Mexico's culinary bonanza into your kitchen with minimum fuss. They reveal the many faces of Mexican cuisine, in recipes ranging from well-known Gazpacho (page 58) to such regional specialties as Yucatecan Pork in Banana Leaves (page 72). Here, too, you'll discover the lighter side of Mexican cooking in such unexpected delights as an oil-free Merida Salad (page 56) and an all-vegetable Chili Verde (page 88).

To enhance your adventures with Mexican cooking, each recipe includes helpful preparation and cooking times, as well as detailed nutritional information. You'll also find menu suggestions, a shopping guide to Mexican ingredients, and special features that focus on unique aspects of the cuisine.

An Ancient Cuisine

Like other great cuisines, Mexican cooking is a product of both culture and regional agriculture. Mexico's historical roots feature prominently in today's diet, as well.

Mexican cooking combines the foods of two worlds: Indian and Hispanic. The Aztecs, Mayans, Toltecs, and other tribes that contributed so much to Mexico's culture lived on staples native to their land—corn, cocoa, pumpkins, tomatoes, chiles, potatoes, beans, and vanilla. When Spanish invaders arrived in Mexico in the 16th century, they brought foods from their homes in Europe, including livestock, cheeses, orchard fruits, and wheat, along with their own cooking techniques. Blended together, these two rich but different legacies evolved into today's Mexican cuisine.

Geography also played a major role. A land of enormous contrasts in terrain, Mexico ranges from lush valleys and balmy seashores to impenetrable mountains and tropical jungles. Before modern roads cut swaths through the often daunting topography, regions remained isolated from one another, resulting in very different local cuisines.

On the plains of northern Mexico, space for growing wheat and grazing cattle explains why flour tortillas, beef, and dairy cheeses are dietary mainstays there. Along the coasts, each town boasts its own seafood dishes: a Pacific coast town may favor a fish unknown in villages on the Gulf coast. In tropical regions where banana trees grow, the leaves are often used to wrap foods for cooking. Along the Caribbean, culinary exchanges with nearby islands have heightened appreciation of the black bean, while in other areas the pinto bean is preferred.

A Word About Our Nutritional Data

For our recipes, we provide a nutritional analysis stating calorie count; grams of protein, carbohydrates, and total fat; and milligrams of cholesterol and sodium. Generally, the nutritional information applies to a single serving, based on the largest number of servings given for each recipe.

The nutritional analysis does not include optional ingredients or those for which no specific amount is stated. If an ingredient is listed with an option, the information was calculated using the first choice. Likewise, if a range is given for the amount of an ingredient, values were figured based on the first, lower amount.

In cities, geography has less impact on cuisine, but life-style has more. Sophisticated Mexico City boasts many superb restaurants, offering elegant and urbane fare. In such cosmopolitan beach resorts as Acapulco and Mazatlan, dishes with an international flair cater to the tastes of the tourists.

Certain indigenous foods transcend geography, however, and are celebrated in both traditional and contemporary recipes to this day. Throughout Mexico, no single influence on diet is greater than corn's. Ancient Indians revered corn so highly that they believed the gods had molded men from it! Most importantly, corn is needed to make *masa*, a dough of ground lime-soaked kernels (the lime sloughs off the coarse hull) that becomes the basis of tamales and tortillas. But corn is also enjoyed as a fresh vegetable, an ingredient in puddings, and even in a thick beverage known as *atole*.

Another native food, the cocoa bean, bears witness to the importance of history. It was a cup

Turn your kitchen into a genuine tortilleria with a few simple tools. For Corn Tortillas, you shape golden masa dough into balls, which are then flattened in a tortilla press (lower left). Roll out Flour Tortillas by hand. Before serving, toast on a flat comal (upper right), or griddle. Recipes on page 20.

of the world's earliest "cocoa" that the Aztec lords served Cortés. And it was chocolate from the cocoa bean that a nun slipped into a sauce to make the first *mole poblano* centuries ago.

Mealtimes in Mexico

Eating patterns have also influenced Mexican cooking. Understanding the Mexican approach to eating—which is not a pattern of three square meals a day—gives further insight into the country's culinary heritage.

Visitors to Mexico soon discover that the local people are devoted snackers. They can't seem to consume enough *antojitos*, or "little whims," finger foods purchased from street vendors. These snacks, ranging from juicy, sculpted papaya on a stick to hefty burritos, are eaten at various times throughout the day. Creative little dishes, antojitos offer ideas for wonderful snacks and appetizers to serve in your own home.

But antojitos are only a small portion of what a Mexican eats. The day usually starts with *cafe con leche* (coffee and milk) and a *pan dulce* (sweet roll). Later in the morning, a heartier breakfast of eggs, tortillas, and beans is often served. The afternoon brings the most important family meal, known as the *comida Mexicana*. The biggest repast of the day, a formal comida can involve as many as eight courses, followed by a siesta. The day ends with a *cena*, or light supper; in modern cities, this is often the main meal, instead of an afternoon comida. Somewhere between the comida and cena falls a *merienda*, or snack.

It's easy to incorporate any Mexican dish, regardless of when it's served, into an American menu. Or stage an authentic Mexican feast the next time you entertain. For help in composing different kinds of Mexican-inspired meals, see the menu suggestions on pages 8–9.

Preparing Mexican Food at Home

Though it's very adventurous, Mexican cooking can be done easily in your kitchen. No special equipment is needed for the recipes in this book, unless you want to make your own tortillas. If so, you'll need a tortilla press, which you can find in some cookware stores and specialty catalogs.

A traditional Mexican kitchen would be equipped with an iron *comal* for roasting tortillas and chiles, a stone *metate* and *mano* for grinding and mulling corn, a *molcajete* for blending spices

and salsas, and a *molinillo* for frothing hot chocolate. You'll need only a heavy, uncoated frying pan and a blender or food processor to do these jobs.

Earthenware pots (*ollas*) and casseroles (*cazuelas*) are also common cooking utensils, as well as popular mementos of Mexican trips. Use any low-fire glazed pottery with caution: it can leach unacceptable levels of lead when liquid or acidic foods are placed in it. To be on the safe side, use this kind of pottery only for dry foods, such as breads, tortilla chips, or whole fruits. If you're concerned about a particular piece of pottery, find a local lab that will test it for leachable lead.

Shopping for Mexican Ingredients

Expect a visual feast when you encounter the colorful array of produce in a Mexican market. From sun-dappled mangoes to fresh and dried chiles, it's a brilliant world of tastes and textures.

Throughout this book, we recommend using authentic Mexican ingredients where possible. Fortunately, the increasing number of Hispanic markets in cities throughout the United States makes shopping for Mexican ingredients convenient.

If a specialty ingredient is not readily available, simply use the alternative suggested in the recipe. Locating such common Mexican ingredients as beans, cilantro, and dried or canned chiles usually requires nothing more than a visit to a well-stocked grocery store.

Chiles

The chile pepper has been called the world's most popular flavoring, and it's typically associated with Mexican food. Nearly 200 known varieties alone are grown in Mexico. The recipes in this book call for only a few of the most common. If you're lucky enough to find or grow the other varieties listed here, this guide will help you use them.

In North America, many people think of chile peppers only as a hot seasoning. Contrary to this notion, Mexican cooks use chiles to impart subtle flavor, rather than tongue-searing heat. Understanding the chiles used in Mexican cooking helps produce a more authentic taste and tolerable heat level.

The heat in chiles is concentrated in a volatile oil called capsaicin, found in the interior ribs where the seeds are attached. By removing the ribs and seeds, you can reduce the heat of the chile.

(Continued on page 10)

Mexican Menus

Planning a special occasion brunch? Need ideas for a barbecue extravaganza? What about a light and easy luncheon? The menus below showcase flavorful Mexican recipes in both traditional and unexpected combinations. Intended to whet your appetite, our menus suggest only a few possibilities. Let your imagination roam whenever you want to entertain with a Mexican accent!

CARNITAS FIESTA FOR TEN

Have your guests build their own carnitas platters for a carefree party idea. They roll savory meat and beans into warm tortillas and add finishing touches of lively salsas and crumbled cheese. A selection of traditional accompaniments makes this menu a Mexican celebration!

Guacamole (page 44)
Fried Tortilla Chips (page 41)
Crisp Raw Vegetables for dipping
Carnitas Fiesta (page 37)
Merida Salad (page 56)
Agua Fresca (page 122)

A SAMPLER OF MEXICAN FAVORITES

Eating Mexican food in a restaurant is always fun, but you can enjoy the same food at home, as well. For easy organization, make the enchiladas, salsa, and flan ahead of time. The tacos are quickly assembled. Only the chiles rellenos require last-minute cooking.

Margaritas (page 124)
Salsa Fresca (page 48)
Water-crisped Tortilla Chips (page 41)
Shredded Beef Enchiladas (page 25)
Roast Chicken Tacos (page 21)
Basic Chiles Rellenos (page 33)
**Refried Beans (page 89) and
Mexican Rice (page 92)**
Orange Flan (page 119)

MEXICAN RANCHERA BARBECUE

Taste the good life of a true Mexican cowboy ranch when you serve this menu. Share the festive feeling by doubling or tripling each recipe to feed a crowd: it's easy to do with these recipes.

**Sangria (page 122), Mexican Beer,
or Sparkling Cider**
Jicama & Fresh Fruit Platter (page 47)
Quick Tamales (page 33)
Avocado Gazpacho (page 58)
Grilled Spareribs (page 71)
Chile Strips with Potatoes (page 85)
Hard Rolls (page 105)
Sweet Tortilla Stack (page 120)

EASY-GOING LATIN PICNIC

Here's a delicious way to enjoy a meal at a relaxed Latin pace: set out an array of cold dishes that can be eaten out-of-hand in any order. Only the soup requires a spoon.

Sangrita (page 122) or Assorted Fruit Juices
Spiced Peanuts (page 41)
Empanadas (page 47)
Spicy Mexican Jerky (page 45)
Gazpacho (page 58)
Cornbread (page 108)
Fresh Papaya & Pineapple
Mexican Wedding Cookies (page 111)

ALL-GRILL MENU

Summer is an outdoor season, and this menu makes the most of outdoor cooking, Mexican style. If you have a covered grill with a temperature gauge, you can even toast the bread for dessert.

Grilled Cheese Appetizer (page 42)
Shrimp with Garlic Butter (page 80)
Grilled Corn (page 85)
Grilled Red Onion Halves
Mexican Bread Pudding (page 120)
**Chilled White Wine or
Sparkling Mineral Water**

CHRISTMAS EVE SUPPER

Like all holidays, Christmas in Mexico is celebrated with spirited gusto and rich tradition. This menu features favorite seasonal dishes.

Mexican Eggnog (page 125)
Large Tamales (page 31)
Christmas Eve Salad (page 56)
Turkey in Mole Sauce (page 76)
White Rice (page 92)
Sweet Cheese Pudding in Syrup (page 121)

TWO-WAY CHILI FOR THE SUPER BOWL

Warm up for the year's big sporting event by serving two kinds of Mexican chili—one with meat and one without. With these hearty choices, you can be sure that everybody wins!

Black Bean Dip (page 44)
Red Chili with Meat (page 66)
Green Chili (page 88)
Spinach Salad with Crisp Red Chiles (page 55)
French Bread or Rolls
Beer & Sodas

A YUCATAN-STYLE DINNER

Along the eastern shore of Mexico, the Yucatan peninsula offers some of the finest cuisine in the country. Equally famous for its Mayan ruins and its tropical beaches, the region is also appreciated for *achiote* seasoning and *pibil* (banana leaf), both of which are used in this menu.

Chilled Fish in Escabeche (page 80)
Yucatecan Pork in Banana Leaves (page 72)
Black Beans (page 89)
Stewed Chayote Squash (page 87)
Papayas, Bananas & Vanilla Ice Cream

DO-AHEAD LUNCHEON FOR SIX

By featuring seviche and tangy green enchiladas on this light menu, you can do all the preparation a day ahead of time. For an easy ending, serve ice cream.

Scallop Seviche (page 50)
Cream Cheese, Crackers & Pepper Jelly
Green Enchiladas with Chicken (page 26)
Sliced Tomatoes & Red Onion with Vinaigrette
Chocolate-Almond Ice Cream (page 113) or purchased ice cream

SOUTH-OF-THE-BORDER SUNDAY BRUNCH

In a true Mexican brunch, eggs usually appear with beans and tortillas. For a unique approach, try this south-of-the-border version of eggs Benedict instead. Start with rich Mexican Hot Chocolate and honey-drenched Sopaipillas. Finish with fresh fruit.

Mexican Hot Chocolate (page 112)
Fresh Orange Juice
Sopaipillas (page 105) & Honey
Eggs Tijuana (page 97)
Fresh Strawberries & Melon

AN ELEGANT SIT-DOWN DINNER FOR FOUR

Treat your favorite friends to an unparalleled repast of contemporary Mexican dishes. Unless they're well acquainted with the spirited cuisine, this menu will surprise them.

Cheese-stuffed Squash Blossoms (page 45)
Asparagus with Tomatillos (page 87)
Salmon with Cilantro Salsa (page 82)
Vermicelli with Vegetables (page 93)
Sautéed Cherry Tomatoes
Spiced Custard (page 117)
Mexican After-Dinner Coffee (page 125)

SUNDAY SOUP SUPPER

Soup and salad with a Mexican flair create a simple, yet filling, menu. Only the avocado needs last-minute touches; everything else can be made ahead.

Avocado with Jalapeño Dressing (page 55)
Menudo (page 61)
Chorizo Bread (page 108)
Cherimoya Ice (page 117)

Although chile heat varies greatly, smaller varieties are generally hotter than larger ones. But heat levels may differ even within the same variety, depending on climate and soil conditions where the chiles were grown. And the human palate varies, too: a chile that's fiery to one person may taste mild to another. In fact, experts rate chile potency on a scale of zero to 120. The common jalapeño pepper (hot by many people's standards) rates only 20, whereas the habanero rates 120. (Now, that's hot!)

Fresh chiles. When selecting fresh chiles from the produce section of your market, make sure they're firm, smooth, and glossy, with no splits or signs of withering. To keep them fresh at home, refrigerate them in a plastic bag for up to 3 days.

When handling fresh chiles, it's best to protect your hands with rubber gloves and avoid touching your face or eyes. Thoroughly wash any skin area that comes into contact with chile oil.

If a burning sensation is caused by eating a chile, suck a lime wedge to neutralize the heat.

To roast and peel fresh chiles for chiles rellenos and other dishes, you need to blister the waxy outer skin. There are three ways to do this. First, if you have a gas range, you can rotate the chiles, one at a time, over the flame until they're charred and blistered (1 to 1½ minutes). Second, you can arrange the chiles on a baking sheet, set them 3 inches below a preheated broiler unit, and broil them, turning often, until blistered (6 to 8 minutes). Finally, to peel a large number of chiles, arrange them slightly apart on baking sheets and roast, uncovered, in a 450° oven, turning several times, until the skin is browned and blistered (20 to 30 minutes).

After blistering chiles by any technique, place them in a plastic bag while they're still warm; twist the bag to close and let the chiles sweat until they're cool enough to handle. Peel off the skins under cold running water; then remove and discard the stems and seeds, if necessary. If you've made them ahead, refrigerate for up to 3 days.

Dried chiles. Dried chiles add a special flavor to numerous Mexican sauces. Look for dried chiles near the spices in Hispanic and well-stocked markets; they should not be cracked or overdry and powdery. Wipe off dusty chiles with a cloth. Most dried chiles will keep indefinitely if stored in a cool, dry place.

Dried chiles are often soaked or ground into powder. Ground chile powder can be found in plastic bags in Hispanic and some specialty food stores; it adds a deep flavor and some heat to chilis,

stews, and sauces. However, don't confuse this product with chili (spelled with a final "i") powder, the commercially prepared spice mixture of seasonings and dried chiles.

Chile Varieties

Chiles may confuse you until you become familiar with them. One name can refer to several different chiles, and one chile may go by different names. Many chiles change names, depending on whether they're dried or fresh.

The lists below can help you sort things out. The first one describes the chiles most commonly found in markets in the United States and used in the recipes in this book. Following is a list of less common chiles that are occasionally available.

Anaheim: fresh and canned. Also called California fresh chile or long green chile, this pointed, 6- to 7-inch-long pepper is bright green and mild to medium-hot in flavor. Many are processed and sold in cans as whole or diced green chiles. Dried Anaheims are usually labeled California or New Mexico dried chiles (page 12).

Ancho: dried. This broad, triangular chile is the dried form of the fresh red poblano chile (page 12). It's most often used in *mole* sauces.

California: fresh and dried. Fresh, this is the Anaheim (above) by a different name. Dried, it's also called New Mexico dried chile (page 12).

Cayenne: dried. Small, thin, and fiery hot in flavor, these chiles are commonly ground into a commercial powder known as ground red pepper or cayenne pepper.

(Continued on page 12)

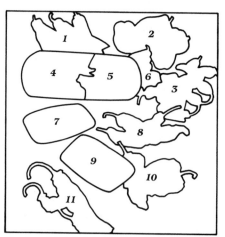

Fresh and dried chiles (shown on facing page): 1) Anaheim, 2) Poblano, 3) Jalapeño (red and green), 4) Chile de arbol, 5) Serrano, 6) Yellow chile peppers, 7) Cascabel, 8) Dried New Mexico, 9) Chipotle, 10) Ancho, 11) Dried pasilla.

Mild to fiery, smooth to wrinkled, bright green to deep mahogany,
chiles in all their variety add distinctive flavor and color to Mexican cooking.
Several of the most popular fresh and dried chiles , including those used in this
book, are pictured here. Diagram on facing page identifies the chiles shown above.

Chile negro: dried. See Pasilla, below.

Chipotle: dried and canned. This is the name of the smoked and dried red jalapeño chile. Chipotles are most often found canned in a vinegar and tomato sauce called *en adobo*. Because flavor is concentrated, they're hotter than fresh jalapeños.

Fresno: fresh. These small, bright green or red chiles are originally from California and are widely used as a substitute for jalapeños (below). They tend to be milder in flavor than other small chiles.

Jalapeño: fresh and canned. From Jalapa in Mexico comes this favorite small hot chile. Fresh red and green jalapeños are easy to find, as are canned and pickled jalapeños.

New Mexico: fresh and dried. This long green or red chile is much like the Anaheim (page 10) when fresh, only slightly hotter in flavor. The dried form (also called dried California chile) is dark red and often found strung into decorative ropes, or *ristras*. Mild to medium-hot in flavor, the dried chiles are often used soaked and puréed in dishes, or ground fine into chile powder.

Pasilla: fresh and dried. This thin, 5- to 7-inch-long chile is dark brown when ripe and black when dried. Pasilla chiles are medium-hot in flavor and are used interchangeably with poblano chiles (below). The dried pasilla is also called chile negro.

Poblano: fresh. Broad, dark green, and mild to medium-hot in flavor, this triangular-shaped chile is popular for chiles rellenos. Dried poblanos are called ancho chiles (page 10).

Serrano: fresh. Another popular and widely available small chile, serranos are darker green, more slender, and hotter than jalapeño or Fresno chiles (above). But all three are often used interchangeably.

The following chiles, not called for in this book, are less common, but you can find most of them in well-stocked Mexican markets.

Cascabel: dried. A round, very hot dried chile, cascabel means "rattle," the sound of seeds heard when the chile is shaken.

Chile de arbol: dried. This chile is similar to the cayenne (page 10).

Guajillo: dried. Brownish orange in color and distinctively fruity-hot in flavor, this chile is called mirasol when fresh.

Güero: fresh. Called the blond chile because of its yellow to pale green color, this chile is fiery hot in flavor and can be used in place of jalapeños or serranos when more heat is desired.

Habanero: pickled. The lantern-shaped chile of the Yucatan, habanero is the hottest chile on the potency scale. Unavailable fresh in this country, it can occasionally be found pickled. In some areas it's called scotch bonnet. Use with caution.

Mirasol: fresh. See Guajillo, below left.

Mulato: dried. Similar to the ancho (page 10), the mulato is the dried form of a large, fleshy green chile (not available fresh in the United States).

Pequin: dried. Tiny round or oval chiles that are fiery hot, pequins can be used in place of cayennes (page 10).

Tepin: dried. Tiny, round, and very hot, these chiles can be used like cayennes or pequins (page 10 and above).

Yellow chile peppers: fresh and pickled. Small, waxy, bright yellow chiles similar in shape and heat to the jalapeños, the group includes Santa Fe grande, caribe, and banana chile peppers. Probably most familiar are canned pickled wax peppers.

Other Specialty Ingredients

Here is a guide to other foodstuffs that give Mexican cuisine its unique and distinctive flavor.

Achiote. Small, brick red achiote seeds come from the annatto tree, native to Mexico. Before use, the seeds must be soaked overnight in water, then ground into a paste. Achiote gives foods a subtle, earthy flavor and deep red color. Look for the seeds, sold in small packets, where spices are displayed in Mexican markets; achiote paste is sometimes available in brick form.

Avocado. Once considered exotic, buttery-textured avocados from California and Florida are now available all year. The bumpy-skinned, dark green Hass can be used interchangeably with the smooth, bright green varieties.

Banana leaves. Ideal natural wrappers for cooking food, sturdy banana leaves can be found refrigerated or frozen (usually in 1-pound packages) in Latin or Southeast Asian markets. Before using, the leaves must be softened. See page 72 for instructions.

Cactus pads. See Nopales, page 15.

Chayote. Grown in Mexico and the United States, this tropical summer squash is pale green and pear shaped, with deeply furrowed skin. Sold in Mexican markets and some produce stores, it's often labeled "mirliton" in southern United States.

Cheese. Many different Mexican cheeses can be found in markets north of the border. For a look at what's available, see page 13.

(Continued on page 15)

Mild & White Mexican Cheeses

A sprinkling of crumbled, tart queso fresco jazzes up a chalupa. The creaminess of asadero enriches a quesadilla. Both cheeses, and others like them, have been made on Mexican cattle ranches since the 16th century. Mild and uncomplicated, these cheeses add just the right accent to dishes without overwhelming other flavors.

Today, many cheese makers in the United States produce these country-style Mexican cheeses for our market. If you're fortunate enough to find such cheeses in your area, they can add delicious authenticity to your Mexican meals. However, many of our own cheeses, such as jack and domestic Parmesan, are good substitutes.

This guide will help you shop for and use Mexican cheeses and creams. Look for them in supermarkets in Hispanic neighborhoods or in Latin grocery stores.

To mail-order Mexican cheeses and creams, contact Cacique Cheese Co., Box 729, City of Industry, CA 91747; phone (818) 961-3399.

Fresh Cheeses

Made from pressed or ground cow's milk curds, these simple cheeses are aged for only a few days, except for cotija, which is aged for at least 3 months. They have a clean, fresh taste and aroma, reminiscent of cottage or farmer's cheese. Because they spoil quickly, these cheeses must be stored in the refrigerator. They can be heated lightly, but if overcooked, they will become rubbery.

Adobera takes its name from its adobe-brick shape: the curds are pressed and drained in a rectangular mold. Slice and eat it like jack cheese.

Cotija is also called *queso añejo* (aged cheese) or *queso seco* (dry cheese). It's aged longer than other fresh cheeses—at least 3 months—and gains sharper flavor as a result. Use it like Parmesan, grated or crumbled over dishes before serving. Or use it in place of queso fresco (above right) when a tangier taste is desired. Grated Romano or Parmesan are good substitutes.

Cuajada means curd. As a cheese, it's similar to queso fresco (above right) but more moist and tender. Sprinkle slices with herbs or orange peel, and eat.

Panela, a simple cheese of drained clotted curds, tastes much like dry cottage cheese. Use it as you would queso fresco (below).

Queso fresco, the most widely distributed Mexican cheese, has a texture similar to farmer's cheese. Slice or coarsely shred it to eat alone; or crumble it on tacos, enchiladas, chalupas, chiles rellenos, eggs, hot beans, or salads. A mild feta cheese substitutes well.

Cooked Cheeses

Made with melted curds, each cooked cheese develops its own character, depending on how it's handled, shaped, and aged. In flavor and texture, cooked cheeses parallel our own jack, mozzarella, and Longhorn Cheddar. They soften and melt smoothly when cooked.

Like fresh cheeses, they should be stored in the refrigerator.

Asadero takes its name from *asado,* the Spanish word for "roasted." It melts smoothly and is usually sold in slices or as a long log. Some cheesemakers stretch and roll it into balls (called *queso Oaxaca,* after the state) that pull apart into strands, like string cheese. Use it in quesadillas, chiles rellenos, chile con queso, or enchiladas. Or dice and add it to hot soups.

Chihuahua is named for the northern state where it originated. Sometimes called *queso menonita,* it ranges from creamy (like Münster) to firm (like Cheddar). Use it as suggested for asadero (above).

Heavy Creams

Two smooth, heavy creams used in Mexican cooking, *crema* and *jocoque,* are also available where Hispanic foods are sold. Some brands are as thick and creamy as crème fraîche; others are creamy but thin. Use in place of sour cream (crema is best for desserts). Sold in jars, these creams must be refrigerated.

*Latin markets in cities north of the border offer an abundance
of Mexican ingredients. Many regular supermarkets also carry such items as dried
beans, tomatillos, jicama, and Mexican chocolate. Diagram on facing page
identifies the specialty ingredients shown above.*

...Other Specialty Ingredients

Cherimoya. This delicious tropical fruit, grown both in the United States and Mexico, has green, textured skin and smooth, custardlike flesh. Enjoy it raw (the large black seeds are edible) or use it in custards, chiffons, or sorbets. Cherimoya is available December through May.

Chocolate. One of Mexico's favorite ingredients, chocolate is made from indigenous cocoa beans. See page 112 for a full description.

Chorizo. This spicy Mexican-style sausage can be purchased from butchers or made at home (page 39). Spanish chorizo is slightly drier but can be used instead.

Cilantro. Also called coriander or Chinese parsley, this pungent green herb gives distinctive flavor to innumerable Mexican dishes. It can be found fresh the year around in most supermarkets.

Dried beans. Pinto, red kidney, and black beans are commonly used in Mexican cooking. Pinto and kidney beans need to be soaked before cooking. Look for packaged dried beans in any supermarket.

Dried corn husks. Sold in packages in Mexican markets, dried corn husks (*hojas de maiz*) from large ears of field corn are an essential ingredient for making tamales. They must be soaked before use. Fresh corn husks, cleaned of silk, work just as well for small tamales.

Epazote. Known sometimes as wormseed or goosefoot, this medicinal-tasting herb is used widely in Mexican cooking, especially in preparing black beans (it's reputed to ease digestion). Look for dried epazote in Mexican markets near other dried herbs; fresh leaves are harder to find, but check specialty seed catalogs to grow your own.

Hominy. These large yellow or white corn kernels have been soaked in lime to remove their husks. Look for dried or frozen hominy in Mexican markets or use widely available canned hominy.

Jicama. This bulky, brown-skinned root vegetable looks like a large turnip, but its crisp white flesh tastes like a slightly sweet water chestnut. It's widely available in grocery stores and produce markets.

Lard. Homemade, freshly rendered pork lard is the Mexican cook's fat of choice. Since the flavorless processed blocks available in American markets are a disappointing substitute for fresh lard, we call for vegetable oil instead in most of this book's recipes.

Mango. One of the most popular fruits in Mexico, mango has a peachlike taste and flowery aroma. Imported mangoes appear in our markets sporadically from January through August. To slice a mango, score the skin lengthwise in 4 to 6 places and pull it off. Cut the flesh from each side of the pit; then slice or cut into chunks.

Masa. Masa is the corn-flour dough used to make tortillas and tamales, sometimes available fresh from Mexican delicatessens or tortilla factories. You can easily make masa from dehydrated masa flour, available at most supermarkets. A similar product, called corn tortilla flour, is available at some specialty food stores.

Nopales (cactus pads). The pads of the prickly pear cactus—nopales—are eaten both fresh and canned throughout Mexico. For a full description, turn to page 103.

Pepitas. Pepitas are raw, unsalted pumpkin seeds usually available in health food stores. In Mexico, the seeds are generally ground into sauces.

Piloncillo. This is unrefined sugar that is shaped into small brown cones and is found mainly in Mexican markets. It's used to sweeten some desserts, as well as Mexican coffee (page 125). Wrapped airtight, the cones will keep indefinitely.

Tomatillo. Despite their resemblance, small, green, husk-wrapped tomatillos are not a variety of tomato. Their tart flavor distinguishes many green sauces, and they're sold both fresh and canned in some well-stocked supermarkets. When using fresh tomatillos, remove the papery husk and stem; then rinse each fruit to remove its sticky coating.

Tortillas. Tortillas are Mexico's omnipresent flat bread. For a discussion of both corn and flour tortillas, see page 17.

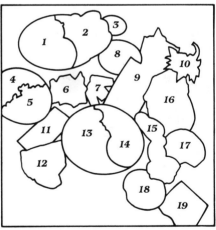

Specialty ingredients (shown on facing page): 1) Mangoes, 2) Nopales, 3) Pepitas, 4) Black beans, 5) Pinto beans, 6) Mexican chocolate, 7) Piloncillo, 8) Dried hominy, 9) Dried corn husks, 10) Epazote, 11) Achiote brick, 12) Achiote seeds, 13) Tomatillos, 14) Avocados, 15) Chayotes, 16) Dehydrated masa flour, 17) Jicama, 18) Queso fresco, 19) Cotija cheese.

Mexican Favorites

Picture a crisp, crescent-shaped taco, a steaming burrito bursting with guacamole, and tender chicken enchiladas drizzled with zesty sauce. Sound deliciously familiar?

We call such specialties "Mexican Favorites" because of their enduring and widespread popularity. Also on the list are crunchy, saladlike tostadas and soft, spicy tamales, along with flautas, chimichangas, chiles rellenos, chilaquiles, and quesadillas.

With the help of this chapter, you can try out basic recipes as well as unusual variations for these versatile dishes. You'll have the chance to master techniques and vary flavors as you see fit. We begin with an in-depth introduction to the tortilla—the cornerstone ingredient of Mexican meals and basic to most of the Mexican favorites.

TORTILLAS

Like most of the world's great inventions, tortillas were born of necessity. Blessed with abundant corn and in need of a nutritious, easily transported staple, ancient Mexicans created *masa*, a moist dough made from ground lime–soaked corn kernels (the lime sloughs off the kernel's coarse skin). The masa was then slapped into thin discs and toasted briefly. The result? Good-tasting, portable tortillas.

Mexico's distinctive flat bread, a tortilla can be stacked, rolled, folded, torn, cut, or eaten as is. It's delectable soft or fried, toasted or baked. It stores well and can be made ahead and reheated. A testament to the ingenuity of the tortilla is its long history. For many centuries, it has continued to be the mainstay of the Mexican diet.

Today, tortillas are made both by hand in time-honored fashion and by machine. Though both methods can give excellent results, the quality of a freshly handmade tortilla cannot be matched commercially.

For home use, your choices are to purchase either packaged corn tortillas (excellent quality is available in the United States) or dehydrated masa flour (corn tortilla flour) for making your own. Flour tortillas—a specialty of northern Mexico—are also widely available, as well as easily made by hand. All the recipes in this book specify whether to use corn or flour tortillas.

Buying & Storing Tortillas

Look for packaged tortillas in the ethnic section of your supermarket; frozen tortillas and prefolded corn tortillas labeled "taco shells" are also available. Sizes vary: for example, flour tortillas range from 6 to 10 inches across. Corn tortillas are usually about 6 inches in diameter.

Check unfrozen tortillas to be sure they are flexible and tender by gently bending the package; edges should not be dry or cracked.

Tortillas will keep for a few months in a home freezer, but they lose flavor and moisture after several days in the refrigerator. After opening the package, rewrap unused tortillas well in plastic or foil. To thaw, gently separate, brush off ice crystals, and lay flat at room temperature for 5 minutes.

Heating & Serving Tortillas

Corn and flour tortillas play diverse roles in the recipes throughout this book. But tortillas are also delicious on their own, served as a snack or with a meal. Though fresh tortillas are soft when you buy them, they become even more tender and flexible when heated. Or they can be fried until crisp and served as a crunchy accompaniment with soups and salads.

Follow these simple guidelines for heating and serving tortillas. Be sure not to heat tortillas longer than necessary to soften and warm them thoroughly, or they will become hard and brittle.

To heat or reheat, remove tortillas from package (thaw, if frozen). If tortillas are dry and a little hard, dip your hand in water and rub tortillas lightly. Stack tortillas, wrap in foil, and heat in a 350° oven until hot (about 15 minutes). Or place tortillas, one at a time, on an ungreased frying pan or griddle over medium-high heat; cook, turning frequently with tongs, until soft and hot (about 30 seconds per tortilla).

To microwave, seal stacked tortillas in plastic wrap (or puncture several holes in plastic packaging) and microwave on **HIGH (100%)** for 6 or 7 seconds per tortilla.

To toast, place tortillas on a grill 3 to 4 inches above medium-hot coals or on an ungreased frying pan or griddle over medium-high heat. Cook, turning once or twice, until very hot and slightly blistered (about 1 minute per tortilla).

To fry, pour oil to a depth of ½ inch into a wide frying pan and heat to 350°F on a deep-frying thermometer. Cook tortillas, one at a time, turning once with tongs, until crisp and golden brown (about 1 minute). Drain on paper towels.

To serve warm, wrap tortillas in a napkin and serve in a basket or covered dish. If desired, spread with butter or margarine before serving; then fold or roll to keep melted butter inside.

To keep hot for several hours, seal warm tortillas in foil; wrap in a cloth and several layers of newspaper.

Making Tortillas

Making your own tortillas and enjoying their superior taste and texture isn't difficult if you follow the simple recipes on page 20.

To make corn tortillas, purchase dehydrated masa flour (corn tortilla flour) from a Mexican grocery or gourmet store (most supermarkets carry it as well). Do not substitute cornmeal. Because dehydrated masa flour is also needed for preparing tamales (page 31) and other dishes, you may want to buy it in bulk. Store it in an airtight container in a cool, dry place.

Both corn and flour tortillas can be patted into shape by hand, but the technique is most successfully learned at a Mexican mother's knee. A rolling pin will also do. Or, for quick and excellent results with corn tortillas, purchase a tortilla press (pictured on page 6) at a cookware store.

Tortillas Every Shape

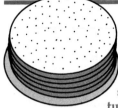

An all-purpose ingredient, the tortilla is one of the great inventions of the world's cuisines. Not only does it add texture, nourishment, and flavor to countless recipes, but it can also be shaped into an edible container.

Using simple molds, you can transform tortillas into portable bowls, baskets, and cones for filling and eating. Or, left flat, the tortilla makes a flexible lid to both lock in heat and serve as a wrapper for the food it covers. Sample our suggestions below or experiment with your own ways to enjoy these versatile tortilla containers. All are pictured on the facing page.

Tortilla Bowls

Pour **salad oil** to a depth of 2 inches into a deep 3- to 4-quart pan and heat to 375°F on a deep-frying thermometer.

Use a can opener to puncture 4 holes in bottom of an empty 10 ½-ounce soup can. Punch 4 more holes in side, just above bottom.

Place a **corn tortilla** (6-inch diameter) in hot oil. Holding open end of can with tongs, immediately set punctured end of can on center of tortilla, pushing it down into oil. Cook tortilla until crisp (about 30 seconds). Lift out can with tortilla, draining excess oil back into pan. Let cool slightly; ease tortilla off and drain on a paper towel. Repeat for desired number of tortillas, maintaining oil temperature at 375°F.

If made ahead, wrap airtight and store at room temperature until next day. To reheat, place bowls in a single layer on baking sheets and warm in a 350° oven for 5 minutes. Fill with thick chili, stew, or beans, or use as a container for Guacamole (page 44).

Tortilla Baskets

Pour **salad oil** to a depth of 2 inches into a deep 3- to 4-quart pan and heat to 375°F on a deep-frying thermometer. Prepare a 10 ½-ounce soup can as directed for **Tortilla Bowls** (above).

Place a **flour tortilla** (7- to 9-inch diameter) in hot oil. Cook for a few seconds to soften; turn with tongs and push into oil with can as directed for Tortilla Bowls. When tortilla begins to crisp (about 30 seconds), lift out can, gently pushing down with a spoon to free tortilla. Continue cooking until crisp and golden (about 1 more minute). Drain on a paper towel. Repeat for desired number of tortillas, maintaining oil temperature at 375°F.

If made ahead, store and reheat as directed for Tortilla Bowls. Use for tostadas or fill with salads or Eggs Tijuana (page 97).

Tortilla Cones

To make each cone mold, fold a 10-inch square of foil into a triangle; then loosely roll into a cone.

Pour **salad oil** to a depth of 1 inch into a deep 10- to 12-inch frying pan and heat to 375°F on a deep-frying thermometer. Roll a **flour tortilla** (7- to 9-inch diameter) into a cone and secure with a wooden skewer; insert foil cone. Place in oil and cook, turning with tongs, until crisp and golden (about 1 minute). Lift cone from oil, draining briefly into pan, and set on a paper towel. Repeat for desired number of cones, maintaining oil temperature at 375°F. When cool enough to handle, remove foil and skewer.

If made ahead, store and reheat as directed for Tortilla Bowls (at left). Fill with Ground Beef Filling (page 21) or other meat fillings (page 39).

Tortilla Lids

Stack desired number of **flour tortillas** (7- to 9-inch diameter) and wrap in foil. Heat in a 350° oven for 15 minutes; or wrap in plastic and microwave on **HIGH (100%)** for 6 or 7 seconds per tortilla.

Serve each tortilla draped over bowls of thick chili or beans. Or prepare individual **Chorizo-Cheese Appetizers:** for each serving, combine ¼ cup cooked, crumbled **Chorizo** (page 39) or purchased chorizo sausage and ½ cup diced **jack cheese** in a small ovenproof bowl. Bake in a 400° oven until cheese is melted (about 8 minutes); top bowl with a warm tortilla. Spoon chorizo mixture into tortilla lid and roll up.

Per serving: 407 calories, 24 g protein, 16 g carbohydrates, 27 g total fat, 84 mg cholesterol, 495 mg sodium

Crisp baskets, bowls, and cones, molded from tortillas, come in handy for serving Guacamole (recipe on page 44), cooked beans, or thick stews. Or drape a warm tortilla over a bowl of Chorizo-Cheese Appetizers (recipe on facing page) and use as a wrapper for the bowl's contents. To shape tortillas, see the instructions on the facing page.

Tortillas de Maíz

CORN TORTILLAS

Pictured on page 6

Preparation time: About 30 minutes
Cooking time: About 1½ minutes per tortilla

Use this method to make either 6-inch tortillas for regular use in recipes or small 4-inch tortillas for appetizers.

> **2 cups dehydrated masa flour (corn tortilla flour)**
> **1¼ to 1⅓ cups warm water**

In a bowl, mix masa flour with enough of the warm water to make dough hold together well. Shape into a smooth ball. Divide into 12 equal pieces for 6-inch tortillas or into 24 equal pieces for 4-inch tortillas, and roll each piece into a ball. Cover with a damp paper towel.

To shape with a tortilla press, cover bottom half of press with wax paper and place a ball of dough on paper, slightly off center, toward hinge end of press. Lay another piece of wax paper on dough and close press tightly. Open press; peel off top paper. Repeat for remaining dough, stacking tortillas between pieces of wax paper.

To shape with a rolling pin, place a ball of dough between 2 pieces of wax paper; flatten slightly with your hand. Lightly run rolling pin over dough several times. Flip dough and paper over and roll out into a 4- to 6-inch circle. Carefully peel off top paper. Repeat for remaining dough, stacking tortillas between pieces of wax paper.

To make a perfectly shaped tortilla, use a knife to trim edges. Or cut dough into a circle with end of a 2-pound coffee can.

To cook, place a heavy, uncoated 10- to 12-inch frying pan or griddle over medium-high heat. When pan is hot, lift tortilla, supporting it with paper, and turn over into pan. At once, peel off paper. Cook tortilla until bottom is flecked with brown (about 30 seconds). With a wide spatula, flip tortilla over and cook for 1 more minute; remove from pan and cover with foil. Repeat for remaining tortillas.

Serve immediately. If made ahead, let cool, wrap airtight, and refrigerate or freeze. If desired, wrap tortillas in foil and reheat (thawed, if frozen) in a 350° oven for about 15 minutes. To reheat in a microwave, wrap in plastic and microwave on **HIGH (100%)** for 6 or 7 seconds per tortilla. Makes 1 dozen 6-inch or 2 dozen 4-inch tortillas.

Per tortilla: 68 calories, 2 g protein, 14 g carbohydrates, 1 g total fat, 0 mg cholesterol, 1 mg sodium

Tortillas de Harina

FLOUR TORTILLAS

Pictured on page 6

Preparation time: About 30 minutes
Cooking time: About 2 minutes per tortilla

Introduced to Mexico by the Spanish in the 16th century, wheat flour was quickly translated by the Mexicans into tortillas. However, flour tortillas have never matched corn in popularity. They're consumed mainly in northern Mexico, where they were created.

> **3 cups all-purpose flour**
> **2 teaspoons baking powder**
> **¾ teaspoon salt**
> **About 1 cup warm water**

Stir together flour, baking powder, and salt. Gradually stir in enough of the warm water to form a crumbly dough; work dough with your hands until it holds together. Turn out onto a board and knead until smooth. Divide into 12 equal pieces and shape each into a smooth ball. Cover lightly with plastic wrap and let rest for 15 minutes.

For each tortilla, flatten a ball into a 4- or 5-inch patty; roll into about a 9-inch round, working from center to edges. Turn tortilla often, stretching dough as you carefully peel it off board.

As each tortilla is shaped, place in a heavy, uncoated wide frying pan or griddle over medium-high heat. Almost immediately, tiny blisters should appear. Turn tortilla and immediately press a wide spatula gently but firmly all over top. Blisters will form over most of surface as you press. Turn tortilla again and press until blisters turn golden brown; tortilla should remain soft. If tortilla sticks or scorches, reduce heat.

Stack tortillas as cooked in a folded cloth towel inside a plastic bag; close bag and let tortillas steam.

Serve tortillas as soon as they are soft. If made ahead, let cool, remove from bag, and wrap airtight; refrigerate or freeze. Reheat as directed for Corn Tortillas (at left). Makes 1 dozen 9-inch tortillas.

Per tortilla: 114 calories, 3 g protein, 24 g carbohydrates, .31 g total fat, 0 mg cholesterol, 209 mg sodium

TACOS

Mexico's most popular culinary export must surely be the taco. It's a rolled or folded tortilla that can be stuffed with an almost endless variety of meats, poultry, fish, beans, vegetables, and condiments. In Mexico, tacos are usually served hot and soft as snacks, purchased from street vendors and eaten out-of-hand. North of the border, the most popular version is a crescent-shaped fried taco made with a ground beef filling. There is no single recipe or method for tacos, so start with our basic suggestions and then add variations if you like.

Basic Tacos

Preparation time: About 30 minutes
Cooking time: About 15 minutes

Here's an all-purpose recipe for fried tacos. You can try other fillings instead of ground beef (see page 39 for suggestions) or make Soft Tacos (recipe follows).

> Ground Beef Filling (recipe follows)
> Salad oil
> 12 corn tortillas (6-inch diameter)
> Garnishes (suggestions follow)

Prepare Ground Beef Filling and keep warm.

Pour oil to a depth of ½ inch into a wide frying pan and heat to 350°F on a deep-frying thermometer. When oil is hot, add a tortilla and cook until soft (about 10 seconds). Using tongs, fold in half; hold slightly open and continue to cook, turning once, until crisp (about 1 more minute). Repeat for remaining tortillas, adding more oil as necessary. Drain on paper towels.

Spoon 2 to 3 tablespoons of the filling into each taco shell. Offer garnishes to spoon on individual servings. Makes 6 servings (2 tacos each).

Ground Beef Filling. Crumble 1 pound **lean ground beef** into a wide frying pan over medium-high heat. Add 1 medium-size **onion,** chopped, and 2 cloves **garlic,** minced or pressed. Cook, stirring often, until meat is browned and vegetables are soft (about 10 minutes). Pour off fat.

Stir in 1½ teaspoons **chili powder,** ½ teaspoon *each* **dry oregano leaves** and **paprika,** ¼ teaspoon *each* **ground cumin** and **pepper,** ½ cup **Mild Chile Sauce** (page 49) or canned tomato sauce, and 2 teaspoons **Worcestershire.** Simmer until thickened (about 5 minutes).

Garnishes. Choose from the following, arranged in separate bowls: 2 or 3 small **tomatoes,** diced; 1 cup (4 oz.) shredded **Cheddar cheese;** 1 cup shredded **lettuce;** 1 **avocado,** diced; **sour cream;** and **Salsa Fresca,** homemade (page 48) or purchased.

Per serving: 689 calories, 25 g protein, 43 g carbohydrates, 48 g total fat, 82 mg cholesterol, 357 mg sodium

SOFT TACOS

Prepare **Ground Beef Filling** as directed for **Basic Tacos** (at left).

In an ungreased frying pan, heat 12 **corn or flour tortillas,** one at a time, over medium-high heat, turning often, until soft (about 30 seconds per tortilla). Keep warm. Spoon filling down center of each tortilla and garnish as directed; roll up to eat. Makes 6 servings (2 tacos each).

Per serving: 568 calories, 25 g protein, 43 g carbohydrates, 34 g total fat, 82 mg cholesterol, 357 mg sodium

Tacos de Pollo Asado
ROAST CHICKEN TACOS

Preparation time: About 25 minutes

For a quick and tasty supper, build your own soft taco with purchased roast chicken and other easily assembled ingredients.

> 8 flour tortillas (7- to 9-inch diameter)
> Salsa Fresca (page 48) or purchased salsa
> 1 whole roasted chicken (about 2 lbs.)
> 1 ripe avocado, pitted, peeled, and thinly sliced
> 1 to 2 tablespoons lemon juice
> 2 green onions (including tops), thinly sliced
> 2 cups (8 oz.) shredded Cheddar cheese
> Fresh cilantro (coriander) sprigs

Stack tortillas, wrap in foil, and heat in a 350° oven for 15 minutes. Meanwhile, prepare Salsa Fresca.

Place chicken on a platter or cutting board. Moisten avocado with lemon juice. Arrange avocado, green onions, cheese, cilantro, and salsa in small bowls around chicken. Place warm tortillas in a basket.

For each serving, tear or cut off pieces of chicken and place in a tortilla. Add garnishes to taste and fold tortilla to enclose. Makes 4 servings (2 tacos each).

Per serving: 847 calories, 60 g protein, 53 g carbohydrates, 43 g total fat, 178 mg cholesterol, 812 mg sodium

From the Gulf of Mexico comes the inspiration for Tostadas de Jaiba (recipe on page 37), a crisp tortilla piled high with beans, cheese, lettuce, succulent crabmeat, and toppings. Fresh Tomatillo Salsa (recipe on page 49) adds a finishing touch. Vary this or any other tostada by substituting chicken or meat for the crab.

Flautas
FLUTE-SHAPED TACOS

Preparation time: About 45 minutes to 4½ hours (time varies with filling used)
Cooking time: About 15 minutes

In Spanish, *flauta* means flute, as suggested by the cylindrical shape of these fried tacos. Extra-long flautas, often sold by street vendors in Mexico, are made by overlapping two tortillas.

Eating flautas is fun but sometimes can be messy. To keep filling from spilling out, wrap one end of flauta well in a paper napkin; eat from the other end.

> **Half-recipe Ground Beef Filling (page 21) or about 1¼ cups meat filling of your choice (page 39)**
> 6 **corn tortillas (6-inch diameter)**
> **Salad oil**
> **Chopped onion (optional)**
> **Salsa Fresca, homemade (page 48) or purchased (optional)**

Prepare Ground Beef Filling and keep warm.

In an ungreased frying pan or griddle, heat tortillas, one at a time, over medium-high heat, turning once, until flexible (about 10 seconds per side). Remove from pan and spoon 2 to 3 tablespoons of the filling down center of tortilla (you may have extra filling); roll up tightly and secure with wooden picks or skewers.

Pour oil to a depth of ½ inch into a wide frying pan and heat to 350°F on a deep-frying thermometer. Using tongs, cook each flauta, turning once, until golden brown (about 30 seconds total). Drain on paper towels. (If you prefer, roll and fry tortillas first, and then spoon in filling.) If desired, offer onion and salsa to add to individual servings. Makes 6 servings.

Per serving: 254 calories, 9 g protein, 21 g carbohydrates, 15 g total fat, 23 mg cholesterol, 108 mg sodium

FLAUTAS GRANDE

Prepare as directed for **Flautas** (above), but prepare an entire recipe of **Ground Beef Filling** (page 21) or use 2½ cups of any meat filling on page 39. Soften 12 **corn tortillas** as directed above. For each flauta, overlap 2 tortillas 4 inches. Spoon about ¼ cup of the filling down each pair of tortillas, roll up, and cook as directed. Makes 6 servings.

Per serving: 439 calories, 17 g protein, 35 g carbohydrates, 26 g total fat, 46 mg cholesterol, 210 mg sodium

Tacos de Pescado
FISH TACOS

Preparation time: About 25 minutes
Cooking time: About 20 minutes

Light, yet spicy, these tacos are typically served in seaside towns in Mexico. Simply poach the fish as directed or use cold leftover mild-flavored fish.

> **Tomatillo Salsa (page 49) or purchased mild green salsa**
> 2 **tablespoons lemon juice**
> 1 **small dried hot red chile**
> 2 **tablespoons chopped fresh cilantro (coriander)**
> 2 **cups regular-strength chicken broth**
> 1 **pound red snapper or other firm white-fleshed fish fillets, 1 inch thick**
> **Salad oil**
> 8 **corn tortillas (6-inch diameter)**
> **About 4 cups shredded lettuce**
> **About ¾ cup sour cream**

Prepare Tomatillo Salsa; cover and refrigerate.

In a 10- to 12-inch frying pan, combine lemon juice, chile, cilantro, and broth. Bring to a boil over high heat. Arrange fillets in broth, overlapping if necessary. Return broth to boiling; reduce heat, cover, and simmer until fish looks just slightly translucent or wet inside when cut in thickest part (about 10 minutes). Drain well; break into 1-inch chunks and keep warm.

Pour oil to a depth of ½ inch into a wide frying pan and heat to 350°F on a deep-frying thermometer. When oil is hot, add a tortilla and cook until soft (about 10 seconds). Using tongs, fold in half; hold slightly open and continue to cook, turning once, until crisp (about 1 more minute). Repeat for remaining tortillas, adding more oil as necessary. Drain on paper towels.

To assemble each taco, place a fried tortilla on a plate; spoon chunks of fish into tortilla and add salsa, lettuce, and sour cream, dividing equally. Makes 4 servings (2 tacos each).

Per serving: 527 calories, 30 g protein, 36 g carbohydrates, 30 g total fat, 61 mg cholesterol, 171 mg sodium

ENCHILADAS

Other Mexican favorites may rival the enchilada in popularity, but few equal it in versatility. Once you've mastered the fundamental technique (not a difficult task), you can create endless versions of enchiladas.

In Mexico, making enchiladas starts by dipping tortillas in sauce, followed by frying them, filling them, and eating them without delay. We have modified the classic method to reduce mess, as well as to allow you to prepare enchiladas ahead of time. By either technique, the crowning touch of an enchilada is a fresh and delicious garnish spooned on at serving time.

Following the easy steps below, you can learn to make a foolproof enchilada. Be careful not to fry the tortillas until they're too crisp—a common mistake. Also, bake the enchiladas just until heated through or they will dry out.

If using a purchased enchilada sauce, prepare according to the directions on the label and thin with water or chicken broth if necessary.

Basic Enchiladas

Preparation time: About 1 hour
Baking time: 20 minutes

For a nutritious, balanced meal with a hearty Mexican flavor, serve these meat enchiladas with rice and beans. For a vegetarian alternative, try Fresh Corn Enchiladas (recipe follows). The chile sauce can be made ahead.

> Red Chile Sauce (recipe follows) or 3 cups canned enchilada sauce, heated
> 3 cups Ground Beef Filling (page 21), Shredded Beef Filling (facing page), or meat filling of your choice (page 39)
> Salad oil
> 12 corn tortillas (6-inch diameter)
> ¾ cup finely chopped onion (optional)
> 1½ cups (6 oz.) jack cheese
> 1½ cups sour cream
> Garnishes (suggestions follow)

Prepare Red Chile Sauce and Ground Beef Filling; set aside.

Pour oil to a depth of ¼ inch into an 8- to 10-inch frying pan over medium-high heat. When oil is hot, cook each tortilla, turning once, just until limp and slightly blistered (about 10 seconds per side). Add more oil as needed. Drain on paper towels.

Spread 1 cup of the sauce in a 10- by 15-inch baking dish; set aside. While tortillas are warm, spoon about ¼ cup of the filling down center of each and sprinkle with about 1 tablespoon of the onion, if desired. Roll tortilla around filling. Place enchiladas, seam sides down, in dish. Cover with remaining sauce and sprinkle with cheese. (At this point, you may cover and refrigerate until next day.)

Bake, uncovered, in a 350° oven until hot in center (20 minutes; 30 minutes if refrigerated). Spoon sour cream over enchiladas and offer garnishes to add to individual servings. Makes 6 servings (2 enchiladas each).

Red Chile Sauce. Place 10 to 12 whole **dried ancho or pasilla chiles** on a baking sheet and toast in a 400° oven until fragrant (3 to 4 minutes). Remove and let cool. Discard stems and seeds; place in a bowl, cover with 3 cups **warm water,** and let stand for 1 hour.

Whirl chiles in a blender with enough of the soaking liquid to moisten. Add remaining liquid; ¼ cup **tomato sauce** or tomato paste; 1 clove **garlic,** minced or pressed; ¼ cup **salad oil;** ½ teaspoon **salt;** 1 teaspoon **dry oregano leaves;** and ¼ teaspoon **ground cumin.** Blend until smooth. Pour into a pan and simmer, uncovered, stirring occasionally, for 10 minutes. Keep warm. If made ahead, cool, cover, and refrigerate for up to a week; freeze for longer storage. Reheat before using. Makes 3½ cups.

Garnishes. Choose from the following, arranged in separate bowls: sliced **ripe olives; onion,** finely chopped; grated or crumbled **cotija cheese** (page 13) or Romano cheese; minced **cilantro** (coriander) and whole **pickled chiles.**

Per serving: 828 calories, 29 g protein, 52 g carbohydrates, 59 g total fat, 96 mg cholesterol, 643 mg sodium

FRESH CORN ENCHILADAS

Prepare as directed for **Basic Enchiladas** (at left), substituting following filling for Ground Beef Filling. In an 8- to 10-inch frying pan, melt 2 tablespoons **butter** or margarine over medium-high heat. Add 2 medium-size **onions,** chopped; cook, stirring, until soft (about 5 minutes). Add 3 cups fresh or frozen thawed **corn kernels,** ½ teaspoon **cumin seeds,** and ¼ cup **water.** Reduce heat to medium, cover, and cook for 5 minutes; uncover and cook, stirring often, until excess liquid has evaporated (about 5 more minutes).

Remove from heat and stir in 1 cup **sour cream,** 1 cup (4 oz.) shredded **jack cheese,** and 1 small can

(4 oz.) **diced green chiles.** Season to taste with **salt.** Makes enough filling for 6 servings (2 enchiladas each).

Per serving: 684 calories, 15 g protein, 61 g carbohydrates, 47 g total fat, 44 mg cholesterol, 542 mg sodium

Enchiladas de Ropas Viejas ✗

SHREDDED BEEF ENCHILADAS

Preparation time: About 2½ hours
Baking time: About 25 minutes

Unlike other enchilada dishes, this one has no sauce. Its moistness comes from a filling of sour cream, chiles, and *ropas viejas*, beef braised until tender enough to shred.

    Shredded Beef Filling (recipe follows)
    Salad oil
1 **small onion, chopped**
2 **large cans (7 oz. *each*) diced green chiles**
½ **teaspoon ground cumin**
1 **tablespoon all-purpose flour**
2 **cups sour cream**
3 **cups (12 oz.) shredded jack cheese**
    Salt
12 **corn tortillas (6-inch diameter)**

Prepare Shredded Beef Filling; set aside.

Meanwhile, in an 8- to 10-inch frying pan, combine 2 tablespoons oil, onion, chiles, and cumin. Cook over medium heat, stirring occasionally, until onion is soft (about 5 minutes). Stir in flour; blend in 1 cup of the sour cream and stir until simmering. Remove from heat and blend in 1 cup of the cheese. Season to taste with salt. Set sauce aside.

Cook tortillas in oil as directed for Basic Enchiladas (facing page).

While tortillas are warm, spoon about ⅓ cup of the sauce and ¼ cup of the shredded beef down center of each. Roll tortilla around filling. Place enchiladas, seam sides down, in a 10- by 15-inch baking pan. (At this point, you may cover and refrigerate until next day.)

Bake, uncovered, in a 375° oven until hot in center (about 20 minutes; 30 minutes if refrigerated). Sprinkle remaining 2 cups cheese evenly on top. Continue baking until cheese is melted (about 5 more minutes).

Offer remaining 1 cup sour cream to spoon on individual servings. Makes 6 servings (2 enchiladas each).

Shredded Beef Filling. Trim and discard most of fat from a 2-pound **boneless beef chuck.** Place in a 5- to 6-quart pan with ¼ cup **water.** Cover and cook over medium heat for 30 minutes. Uncover and cook, turning as needed, until liquid has evaporated and meat is well browned (about 10 minutes).

In a bowl, combine 3 tablespoons **red wine vinegar,** 1½ cups **regular-strength beef broth,** 2 tablespoons **chili powder,** and 1 teaspoon **ground cumin;** pour over meat. Cover and cook until meat pulls apart easily (about 2 more hours). Let cool; then shred and mix with pan juices.

Per serving: 866 calories, 44 g protein, 39 g carbohydrates, 60 g total fat, 158 mg cholesterol, 1,072 mg sodium

Enchiladas de Queso

CHEESE ENCHILADAS

Preparation time: About 30 minutes
Baking time: 20 minutes

Simple yet festive, these enchiladas make a light luncheon entrée to serve with fresh fruit and Sangria (page 122).

    Cheese Filling (recipe follows)
12 **corn tortillas (6-inch diameter)**
    Salad oil
2 **large cans (7 oz. *each*) green chile salsa**
2 **cups (8 oz.) shredded Cheddar cheese**
1 **cup finely shredded lettuce**
2 **medium-size tomatoes, thinly sliced**

Prepare Cheese Filling; set aside. Cook tortillas in oil as directed for Basic Enchiladas (facing page).

Spread a third of the green chile salsa in a 10- by 15-inch baking dish. Spoon about ½ cup of the filling down center of each tortilla; roll tortilla around filling. Place enchiladas, seam sides down, in dish. Cover with remaining salsa and Cheddar cheese. (At this point, you may cover and refrigerate until next day.)

Bake, uncovered, in a 350° oven until hot in center (20 minutes; 30 minutes if refrigerated). Garnish with lettuce and tomatoes. Makes 6 servings (2 enchiladas each).

Cheese Filling. Stir together 3 cups **large curd cottage cheese,** 1 cup (4 oz.) shredded **Cheddar cheese,** 1½ cups finely chopped **green onions** (including tops), and ¼ teaspoon **dry oregano leaves.**

Per serving: 626 calories, 32 g protein, 37 g carbohydrates, 39 g total fat, 75 mg cholesterol, 1,308 mg sodium

Enchiladas Verdes con Pollo

GREEN ENCHILADAS WITH CHICKEN

Pictured on facing page

Preparation time: About 45 minutes
Baking time: About 30 minutes

A light tomatillo sauce adds green color and tangy flavor to these enchiladas; a chicken-chile filling makes them hearty.

Tomatillo Sauce (recipe follows)
4 cups coarsely shredded cooked chicken or turkey
3 cups (12 oz.) shredded jack cheese
1 large can (7 oz.) diced green chiles
1½ teaspoons dry oregano leaves
Salt
Salad oil
12 corn tortillas (6-inch diameter)
1 to 1½ cups sour cream
½ cup chopped fresh cilantro (coriander)
Fresh cilantro (coriander) sprigs
1 or 2 tomatillos, husked and thinly sliced, or 1 lime, thinly sliced

Prepare Tomatillo Sauce; set aside.

In a large bowl, mix chicken, 2 cups of the cheese, chiles, and oregano. Season to taste with salt; set aside.

Pour oil to a depth of ¼ inch into an 8- to 10-inch frying pan over medium-high heat. When oil is hot, cook each tortilla, turning once, just until limp and slightly blistered (about 10 seconds per side). Add more oil as needed. Drain on paper towels.

While tortillas are warm, spoon ½ cup of the chicken mixture down center of each. Roll tortilla around filling. Place enchiladas, seam sides down, in a 10- by 15-inch baking pan. (At this point, you may cover and refrigerate until next day.)

Cover enchiladas with foil and bake in a 350° oven until hot in center (about 20 minutes; 30 minutes if refrigerated). Uncover and top with remaining 1 cup cheese. Continue baking, uncovered, until cheese is melted (about 10 more minutes).

Meanwhile, reheat Tomatillo Sauce. To serve, spoon sauce onto a large rimmed platter (or divide among 6 dinner plates). Set enchiladas on sauce. Top each enchilada with a dollop of sour cream; garnish with cilantro and tomatillo slices. Makes 6 servings (2 enchiladas each).

Tomatillo Sauce. Heat ⅓ cup **salad oil** in a 3- to 4-quart pan over medium-high heat. Add 2 medium-size **onions,** chopped; cook, stirring often, until soft (about 5 minutes).

Stir in 1 large can (7 oz.) **diced green chiles;** 2 cans (13 oz. *each*) **tomatillos,** drained; 1 cup **regular-strength chicken broth;** 3 tablespoons **lime juice;** 2 teaspoons **dry oregano leaves;** and 1 teaspoon **ground cumin.** Bring to a boil; reduce heat and simmer, uncovered, stirring occasionally, for 25 minutes. Whirl sauce in a blender or food processor until smooth. Season to taste with **salt.**

Per serving: 896 calories, 48 g protein, 41 g carbohydrates, 60 g total fat, 150 mg cholesterol, 981 mg sodium

Torta de Enchiladas

TURKEY ENCHILADA STACK

Preparation time: About 30 minutes
Baking time: 1 hour and 20 minutes

Here's a shortcut for making enchiladas—you stack them instead of roll them. At the same time, try ground turkey for a lean alternative to meat.

1 cup Tomatillo Salsa (page 49) or purchased mild green salsa
2 cups (8 oz.) shredded Cheddar cheese
1 pound ground turkey
1 small can (4 oz.) diced green chiles
1 small onion, finely chopped
¾ cup chopped tomatoes
8 corn tortillas (6-inch diameter)

Prepare Tomatillo Salsa. Mix 1½ cups of the cheese with turkey, chiles, onion, ½ cup of the salsa, and ½ cup of the tomatoes. Divide mixture into 7 equal portions.

Lay a tortilla in a shallow pie pan and spread evenly with a portion of the turkey mixture. Continue to layer tortillas and filling, ending with a tortilla. Spread last tortilla with remaining ½ cup cheese, ½ cup salsa, and ¼ cup tomatoes.

Cover enchilada stack with foil and bake in a 400° oven for 40 minutes. Uncover and continue baking until turkey in center is cooked through; cut to test (about 40 more minutes).

Let stand for about 5 minutes; cut into wedges to serve. Makes 5 or 6 servings.

Per serving: 387 calories, 26 g protein, 23 g carbohydrates, 21 g total fat, 90 mg cholesterol, 466 mg sodium

*Light and tangy Enchiladas Verdes con Pollo (recipe on facing page)
presents a chile-laden chicken filling rolled in a crisp tortilla and bathed in a tart
tomatillo sauce. At serving time, top warm enchiladas with dollops of sour cream.
Cilantro and sliced tomatillo add a fitting garnish.*

BURRITOS

These easy-to-eat packages roll many delicious ingredients into one flour tortilla. Below, we offer a variety of burrito fillings and condiments, as well as a delicious oven-fried variation called a chimichanga. Try the vegetable-stuffed burrito for a fresh approach. Or, for a delightful party idea, present the eye-catching Six-foot Burrito.

Basic Burritos

Preparation time: About 25 minutes
Cooking time: About 1½ hours

Pork simmered in red sauce is Mexico's traditional filling for burritos. You can also use Carnitas (page 39) or the milder shredded pork filling used in Oven-fried Chimichangas (facing page).

    1 **pound lean boneless pork butt or shoulder, trimmed of excess fat and cut into 1-inch chunks**
 1½ **cups water**
    4 **large dried New Mexico or California chiles (about 3 oz. *total*) or 3 tablespoons ground chile powder**
    1 **clove garlic, minced or pressed**
   ¾ **teaspoon salt**
   ½ **teaspoon dry oregano leaves**
    1 **tablespoon red wine vinegar**
    4 **to 6 flour tortillas (7- to 9-inch diameter)**
       Garnishes (suggestions follow)

Place meat in a 2- to 3-quart pan over medium-high heat and add water. Bring to a boil; reduce heat, cover, and simmer until meat is tender (about 1 hour). Skim off excess fat.

Remove stems and seeds from chiles, break into pieces, and whirl in a blender until finely ground. Add to pork along with garlic, salt, oregano, and vinegar. Simmer, uncovered, stirring occasionally, until sauce thickens (about 35 minutes).

Meanwhile, wrap tortillas in foil and heat in a 350° oven until hot (about 15 minutes). Or wrap in plastic wrap and microwave on **HIGH (100%)** for 30 to 45 seconds. To serve, spoon pork filling down center of each tortilla and add garnishes as desired. Lap ends of tortilla over filling and fold sides to center, or simply roll up. Makes 4 to 6 servings.

Garnishes. Choose from the following, arranged in separate bowls: 1 cup **sour cream,** Guacamole (page 44), 1 cup (4 oz.) shredded **jack cheese,** and shredded **lettuce.**

Per serving: 572 calories, 27 g protein, 41 g carbohydrates, 36 g total fat, 85 mg cholesterol, 822 mg sodium

Burritos de Verduras
VEGETABLE BURRITOS

Preparation time: About 20 minutes
Cooking time: About 35 minutes

Vegetable lovers will applaud the fresh, spicy, and healthful filling inside these burritos. Offer with Mexican Rice (page 92) and scrambled eggs for an out-of-the-ordinary brunch.

    2 **tablespoons salad oil**
    1 **large onion, chopped**
    2 **large carrots, thinly sliced**
    1 **clove garlic, minced or pressed**
 2½ **teaspoons chili powder**
   ¾ **teaspoon *each* ground cumin and dry oregano leaves**
    4 **medium-size zucchini, diced**
    1 **green or red bell pepper, chopped**
    1 **cup fresh or frozen thawed corn kernels**
    1 **large can (16 oz.) kidney beans, drained**
   12 **flour tortillas (7- to 9-inch diameter)**
       Garnishes (suggestions follow), optional

Heat oil in a wide frying pan over medium-high heat. When oil is hot, add onion, carrots, garlic, chili powder, cumin, and oregano. Cook, stirring, until onion is soft (about 10 minutes). Stir in zucchini, bell pepper, corn, and kidney beans and cook until zucchini is tender-crisp (7 to 8 more minutes).

Divide tortillas into 2 stacks, wrap in foil, and heat for 15 minutes in a 350° oven; or wrap in plastic and microwave on **HIGH (100%)** for 30 to 45 seconds per stack. Spoon filling into tortillas; add garnishes, if desired. Lap ends of tortilla over filling and fold sides to center, or simply roll up. Makes 12 servings.

Garnishes. Choose from the following, arranged in separate bowls: 1 cup **sour cream,** Guacamole (page 44), 1 cup (4 oz.) shredded **jack cheese,** shredded **lettuce,** and chopped **tomatoes.**

Per serving: 400 calories, 14 g protein, 74 g carbohydrates, 6 g total fat, 0 mg cholesterol, 711 mg sodium

Burrito Gigante
SIX-FOOT BURRITO

Preparation time: 3 to 4 hours for salsa and chili; 20 minutes to assemble

This burrito calls for a party. Bring friends together to help assemble and eat the spectacular creation. You'll need a long wooden plank from a lumberyard to use as a base for the burrito.

   Blender Salsa (recipe follows)
 8 cups Chili Colorado (page 66), or 3 large cans (about 30 oz. *each*) chili without beans
 2 cups Guacamole (page 44)
18 flour tortillas (7- to 9-inch diameter)
 2 cups chopped onions
 5 cups (1¼ lbs.) shredded jack or Cheddar cheese
 2 large heads butter lettuce, washed and separated into leaves
 2 cups cherry tomatoes, cut in half
 1 cup thinly sliced green onions (including tops)
 2 cups sour cream

Prepare Blender Salsa; set aside. Prepare Chili Colorado; bring to a boil over medium heat, stirring. Prepare Guacamole; set aside.

   To assemble burrito, overlap tortillas down length of a clean 1 by 12 board, 6 to 7 feet long. Ladle chili down center of tortillas in a 2-inch-wide band. Sprinkle on onions and 3 cups of the cheese.

   Bring one side of tortillas up over filling; then roll to enclose, tucking seam underneath. (It's advisable to have several helpers working down length of burrito.) Tuck lettuce leaves under burrito on both sides; garnish with tomatoes and remaining 2 cups cheese.

   To serve, cut burrito into 3- to 4-inch sections; transfer to individual plates with a wide spatula. Garnish with salsa, green onions, sour cream, and Guacamole. Makes 20 to 24 servings.

Blender Salsa. In a blender or food processor, combine 2 medium-size **tomatoes,** cut into chunks; ½ small **onion;** 3 tablespoons **canned diced green chiles;** 4 teaspoons **distilled white vinegar;** and 1 tablespoon chopped **cilantro** (coriander). Whirl until smooth; season to taste with **salt.**

   If made ahead, cover and refrigerate for up to 2 days. Makes about 2½ cups.

Per serving: 673 calories, 30 g protein, 34 g carbohydrates, 47 g total fat, 108 mg cholesterol, 603 mg sodium

Chimichangas al Horno
OVEN-FRIED CHIMICHANGAS

Preparation time: About 25 minutes
Cooking time: About 1¾ hours
Baking time: 8 to 10 minutes

Usually deep-fried, chimichangas can also be oven-fried with less mess, fuss, and fat. Roll the mild pork filling into regular burritos as well.

   Salsa Fresca (page 48)
 1 pound lean boneless pork butt or shoulder, trimmed of excess fat and cut into 1½-inch cubes
 2 cups water
 2 tablespoons white vinegar
 3 tablespoons canned diced green chiles
 1 clove garlic, minced or pressed
 ¼ teaspoon *each* ground oregano and ground cumin
   Salt
 4 flour tortillas (7- to 9-inch diameter)
 3 tablespoons butter or margarine, melted
1½ cups (6 oz.) shredded jack cheese
 1 cup sour cream

Prepare Salsa Fresca; cover and refrigerate.

   Place meat in a 2- to 3-quart pan. Cover and cook over medium heat to draw out juices (about 10 minutes). Uncover and cook over high heat, stirring often, until liquid has evaporated and meat is well browned.

   Add water to pan, stirring to scrape up browned bits. Bring to a boil over high heat; reduce heat, cover, and simmer until meat is very tender when pierced (1 to 1¼ hours). Uncover and boil over high heat until all liquid has evaporated. Reduce heat to low. Add vinegar, chiles, garlic, oregano, and cumin. Stir to scrape up browned bits; remove from heat.

   Shred meat with 2 forks. Season to taste with salt. (At this point, you may cover and refrigerate for up to 3 days; reheat before using.)

   To assemble each chimichanga, brush both sides of a tortilla with melted butter. Spoon filling down center of tortilla. To enclose, lap ends over filling; then fold sides to center to make a packet. Place chimichangas, seam sides down, in a 9- by 13-inch baking pan. Bake in a 500° oven until golden (8 to 10 minutes).

   Offer salsa, cheese, and sour cream to spoon on individual servings. Makes 4 servings.

Per serving: 664 calories, 37 g protein, 28 g carbohydrates, 44 g total fat, 163 mg cholesterol, 674 mg sodium

Feliz Navidad signals the season for festive foods in Mexico.
Large Tamales (recipe on facing page) are the main attraction on this holiday menu.
Christmas Eve Salad (recipe on page 56), Turkey in Mole Sauce (recipe on page 76),
White Rice (recipe on page 92), and purchased corn tortillas complete the menu.

TAMALES

What a treat to unwrap the hot corn husk on your plate and find a tamale inside! And as you eat it, you enjoy the same delectable entrée that ancient Indians in Mexico consumed for centuries. Called *tamal* in Mexico, these steamed bundles are available there in a variety of sizes and flavors, both sweet and savory.

Tamales are typically wrapped in dried corn husks and cooked by steaming. The husks are usually sold in 8-ounce packages, enough for 50 tamales. We also include recipes using foil or fresh corn husks.

Though tamales are not difficult to make, they do require patience and a free afternoon. Serve regular-size tamales as an appetizer, side dish, or luncheon entrée; large tamales are traditionally reserved for special occasions in Mexico, especially Christmas. Smaller *tamalitos* (page 32) are popular fare at Mexican barbecues.

Basic Tamales

Preparation time: About 5½ hours
Standing time (for corn husks): At least 20 minutes
Cooking time: About 1 hour

Tender and savory tamales appear at many traditional Mexican meals, plumped with a meat or chicken filling. To make tamales for a crowd, double or triple the amount of filling. But prepare masa dough in single batches—it's hard to manage in large amounts.

> Masa Dough (recipe follows)
> Tomatillo Salsa (page 49) or Red Chile Purée (page 48)
> 1 package (8 oz.) dried corn husks
> Carnitas (page 39), Shredded Chicken (page 39), or Shredded Beef Filling (page 25)

Prepare Masa Dough; set aside. Prepare Tomatillo Salsa; cover and refrigerate.

Sort through dried corn husks, discarding silk and other extraneous material. In a large roasting pan, cover husks with warm water and let stand until pliable (at least 20 minutes) or until next day. Drain and pat dry when ready to use.

Prepare Carnitas.

For each tamale, select a wide, pliable husk. Lay flat, with tip pointing away from you. Evenly spread 2 tablespoons of the masa down center of husk, forming a rectangle that's flush with one side of husk, an inch from opposite side, an inch from

bottom, and 3 inches from tip. If husk is not wide enough, use some of the masa to paste another husk onto back of first.

Spoon 2 rounded tablespoons of the filling in center of masa. To enclose filling, fold husk so masa edges meet, wrapping plain part of husk around outside of tamale. Fold bottom end of husk over body of tamale; then fold in tip. Place, seam side down, on a tray; cover with damp paper towels until all are prepared.

To steam, place a rack in a 12- to 14-quart pan and pour in boiling water to a depth of an inch. (Water should not reach tamales; if rack is too low, rest it on 2 small cans.) Stack tamales in steamer, arranging loosely so steam can circulate. Bring to a boil; cover and adjust heat to keep water at a steady boil. Continue to cook, adding boiling water to maintain water level, until masa is firm and does not stick to husk; open one from center of pan to test (about 1 hour).

Serve tamales hot or keep warm in steamer over low heat for up to an hour. To serve, peel off husks and offer salsa to spoon on individual servings. Makes about 15 servings (40 to 50 tamales).

Masa Dough. Whip 1⅓ cups **lard,** butter, margarine, or solid shortening until fluffy. Blend in 4 cups **dehydrated masa flour** (corn tortilla flour); 2 teaspoons **salt,** if desired; and 2⅔ cups **warm water** or regular-strength chicken or beef broth. Mix until dough holds together well. If made ahead, cool, cover, and refrigerate for up to 3 days; bring to room temperature before using.

Per serving: 413 calories, 20 g protein, 23 g carbohydrates, 26 g total fat, 74 mg cholesterol, 201 mg sodium

LARGE TAMALES

Pictured on facing page

Prepare as directed for **Basic Tamales** (at left), but, for each tamale, use 2 large soaked **corn husks** (pasted together with masa dough), ⅓ cup **masa dough** (spread into a 5- by 7-inch rectangle, flush with one side of husk), and ¼ cup **filling.**

Fold as directed for Basic Tamales. To keep husks from splitting, place each wrapped tamale atop another corn husk. Lap sides of husk over center; then fold in ends, tucking one into the other. Steam as directed for about 1 hour and 20 minutes. Makes about 18 large tamales.

Per tamale: 344 calories, 16 g protein, 19 g carbohydrates, 20 g total fat, 62 mg cholesterol, 167 mg sodium

Mucbil-Pollo

TAMALE PIE

Preparation time: About 40 minutes, plus 12 hours soaking time to make achiote paste
Cooking time: About 2½ hours

We found this authentic tamale pie in the Yucatan in Mexico (*mucbil* refers to the cooking style; *pollo* means chicken). Down there, it's cooked in a banana leaf as if it were a giant tamale. We wrap it in foil as a more convenient substitute.

>**Masa Dough, made with chicken broth (page 31)**
> ½ cup **Achiote Paste (page 72)**
> 5 cups **water**
> 4 **chicken bouillon cubes**
> ⅛ teaspoon **anise seeds**
> ½ teaspoon **dry mint leaves**
> **4-pound frying chicken, cut up**
> 2 **medium-size onions, quartered**
> 2 **large tomatoes**, *each* **cored and cut into 6 pieces**
> 4 **hard-cooked eggs, halved lengthwise**
> 24 *each* **green onions (including tops) and radishes**

Prepare Masa Dough; cover and refrigerate.

Prepare Achiote Paste and place in a 6- to 8-quart pan; gradually add a little of the water, stirring until smooth. Add remaining water and bouillon cubes; bring to a boil. Reduce heat and simmer, uncovered, for about 10 minutes. Pour liquid through a fine strainer and return to pan; discard residue.

Add anise seeds and mint leaves to broth; place chicken on top. Cover and simmer, without stirring, for 25 minutes. Add onions and cook, without stirring, for 10 more minutes; add tomatoes and cook, without stirring, for 10 more minutes.

Remove pan from heat; with a slotted spoon, gently lift out chicken and vegetables. When chicken is cool, remove and discard skin and bones; tear meat into bite-size pieces.

Boil broth until reduced to 2 cups, stirring often. Remove from heat.

Spread a third of the dough over bottom and sides of a greased shallow 3-quart casserole. Evenly distribute chicken, onions, tomatoes, and eggs over dough; cover with broth. Shake pan gently to level filling.

Spread remaining dough evenly over top, enclosing filling. Cover tightly with foil and bake on lowest rack of a 425° oven for 30 minutes; remove foil and continue baking until top is golden (1 more hour). Let stand for at least 10 minutes before serving. Garnish with green onions and radishes. Makes 8 servings.

Per serving: 770 calories, 35 g protein, 53 g carbohydrates, 47 g total fat, 242 mg cholesterol, 1,213 mg sodium

Tamalitos de Elote

SMALL FRESH CORN TAMALES

Preparation time: About 1½ hours
Cooking time: About 1 hour

Made with sweet corn, these bite-size tamales are wrapped in fresh corn husks.

> 5 **or 6 medium-size ears of corn in husks (about 5 lbs.** *total***)**
> ¼ **cup lard or solid vegetable shortening, melted**
> 2 **teaspoons sugar**
> **Salt**
> ¾ **cup shredded Longhorn Cheddar cheese**
> ⅓ **cup canned diced green chiles**

With a sharp knife or cleaver, remove about ¼ inch from ends of each ear of corn, cutting through husk, corn, and cob. Peel off husks without tearing them; rinse if soiled. To keep moist, put in plastic bags and seal; set aside. Pull silk from corn and discard; rinse corn.

With a knife or corn scraper, cut kernels from cobs to make 4 cups, lightly packed. Put corn through a food chopper fitted with a fine blade or whirl in a food processor until finely ground. Mix with lard and sugar; season to taste with salt. Stir in cheese and chiles.

For each tamale, select a wide, pliable husk. Center 1⅓ tablespoons of the corn filling near stem (firmer) end. Fold a side of husk over to completely cover filling, then fold over other side. Fold up flexible end to seal. Gently stack tamales, folded ends down, on a rack in a steamer, supporting them against other tamales so ends stay shut.

Steam as directed for Basic Tamales (page 31) until centers are firm to touch; unwrap to test (about 1 hour). Serve at once or keep warm in steamer over low heat for up to an hour.

To freeze, let cool completely. Place in a single layer on baking sheets and freeze; when frozen, transfer to plastic bags and store in freezer for up to 6 months. To reheat, let thaw; then steam as directed for about 15 minutes. Makes 3 to 6 servings (3 dozen tamales).

Per serving: 230 calories, 7 g protein, 22 g carbohydrates, 14 g total fat, 23 mg cholesterol, 149 mg sodium

Tamales Rapidos

QUICK TAMALES

Preparation time: About 1½ hours
Cooking time: About 45 minutes

What makes them *rapidos?* Squares of foil instead of traditional corn husks bundle these tamales. They steam just like the traditional kind, but they're much quicker to prepare.

> 2 cups dehydrated masa flour (corn tortilla flour)
> 1¼ cups regular-strength chicken broth
> Salt
> ½ cup salad oil
> 2 cups cooked turkey or chicken, finely diced
> ½ cup pitted ripe olives, coarsely chopped
> 1 medium-size onion, finely chopped
> ½ cup canned green chile salsa

Cut 30 pieces of foil, each 6 inches square. Stir together masa flour, chicken broth, ½ teaspoon salt, and oil to make a thick paste. Spread about 1½ tablespoons of the paste in a 3-inch square in center of each piece of foil.

In a bowl, mix turkey, olives, onion, and salsa; season to taste with salt. Spoon about 1½ table-spoons of the filling down center of each masa square. Fold foil edges together so masa edges meet; seal all sides. Steam as directed for Basic Tamales (page 31) until masa is firm to touch; unwrap to test (about 45 minutes). Makes about 6 servings (2½ dozen small tamales).

Per serving: 413 calories, 18 g protein, 31 g carbohydrates, 25 g total fat, 36 mg cholesterol, 333 mg sodium

CHILES RELLENOS

Its simple name, which means stuffed chile, gives only a modest description of this luscious Mexican specialty. What you can expect is a picante chile enclosing a savory cheese filling and finished with a golden egg coating. It's not a difficult dish to make if taken in steps: prepare the chiles, filling, and sauce; then, just before you're ready to serve, coat and fry.

Choose either fresh, slender Anaheims or stubby, hotter poblanos for stuffing. Canned green chiles can also be used, but they have a softer texture, which can make them difficult to fill.

Basic Chiles Rellenos

Preparation time: About 20 minutes
Cooking time: About 30 minutes

With this recipe you pair the traditional cheese filling with a light tomato sauce. Serve as a vegetable side dish or as a main course with Mexican Rice (page 92) and a salad.

> 6 medium-size Anaheim or poblano chiles or 1 large can (7 oz.) whole green chiles
> 8 ounces jack cheese
> ⅓ cup all-purpose flour
> 1 tablespoon butter or margarine
> 3 tablespoons chopped onion
> 1 clove garlic, minced or pressed
> 1 large can (15 oz.) tomato purée
> ¼ teaspoon dry oregano leaves
> Salt
> Crispy Egg Coating (recipe follows)
> Salad oil

Roast and peel fresh chiles as directed on page 10. (Use canned chiles as is.) Slit each chile three-quarters down length of one side; pull out ribs and seeds, leaving stem intact.

Cut cheese into six ½-inch-thick pieces slightly smaller than chiles; insert a piece into each chile. Roll chiles in flour, shaking off excess. Set aside.

In a medium-size frying pan, melt butter over medium heat. Add onion and garlic; cook, stirring, until golden (about 10 minutes). Add tomato purée and oregano; season to taste with salt. Reduce heat, cover, and simmer for 15 minutes; keep warm.

Meanwhile, prepare Crispy Egg Coating. Pour oil to a depth of 1½ inches into a wide frying pan and heat to 425°F on a deep-frying thermometer. When oil is hot, hold each chile by its stem and dip into egg coating. (For canned chiles, drop them into egg coating and lift out with 2 forks.) Drop into hot oil and cook, 2 or 3 at a time, until golden on both sides (about 2 minutes total), turning once with a fork and spatula. Drain on paper towels.

Offer hot chiles with tomato sauce to spoon on individual servings. Makes 6 servings.

Crispy Egg Coating. Separate 4 **eggs.** In a large bowl, whip whites with 1 teaspoon **salt** until firm peaks form. Beat yolks until blended; then quickly fold into whites. Use at once.

Per serving: 339 calories, 16 g protein, 16 g carbohydrates, 24 g total fat, 221 mg cholesterol, 920 mg sodium

Chiles Rellenos Picadillo

PICADILLO-STUFFED CHILES

Pictured on facing page

Preparation time: About 55 minutes
Cooking time: About 20 minutes

Sweetness and heat interplay in this special dish
that includes a raisin-meat filling (called *picadillo*),
spicy poblano chiles, and a minted salsa.

>   6 **medium-size poblano chiles**
>   **Minted Salsa (recipe follows)**
>   **Picadillo Filling (recipe follows)**
>   ⅓ **cup all-purpose flour**
>   **Crispy Egg Coating (page 33)**
>   **Salad oil**

Roast and peel chiles as directed on page 10. Prepare Minted Salsa; keep warm. Prepare Picadillo
Filling and fill chiles equally with meat mixture.

Prepare Crispy Egg Coating. Roll chiles in
flour, shaking off excess. Pour oil to a depth of 1½
inches into a wide frying pan and heat to 425°F on
a deep-frying thermometer. When oil is hot, hold
each chile by its stem, dip into egg coating, and
drop into hot oil. Cook chiles, 2 or 3 at a time, until
golden on both sides (about 2 minutes total), turning once with a fork and spatula. Drain on paper
towels.

Spoon salsa on plates and top with chiles.
Makes 6 servings.

Minted Salsa. Heat 1 tablespoon **salad oil** in a
10- to 12-inch frying pan over medium heat. Add
1 cup chopped **onion;** cook, stirring, until soft
(about 5 minutes). Core, seed, and chop enough
ripe **tomatoes** to make 2½ cups. Add to pan with
½ cup chopped fresh or canned **pineapple;**
¼ cup chopped **fresh mint leaves,** tightly
packed; ⅓ cup **raisins;** ¾ cup **tomato juice;** and
1 **chicken bouillon cube.**

Bring mixture to a boil; reduce heat and
simmer, uncovered, stirring occasionally, until
reduced to 3 cups (about 10 minutes). Serve warm.

Picadillo Filling. Crumble 1 pound **ground pork**
into a deep 10- to 12-inch frying pan over medium-
high heat. Add 1 small **onion,** chopped; 2 cloves
garlic, minced or pressed; ½ cup **raisins;** ⅓ cup
each slivered **almonds** and chopped **pecans;** and
2 tablespoons *each* **fresh mint leaves** and **fresh
basil leaves,** minced. Cook, stirring, until meat
is browned (about 15 minutes). Add 1 can (8 oz.)
tomato sauce and stir to blend.

*Per serving: 578 calories, 22 g protein, 39 g carbohydrates,
39 g total fat, 238 mg cholesterol, 993 mg sodium*

OTHER FAVORITES

Included in Mexico's artistry with tortillas are classic quesadillas, chilaquiles (a popular casserolelike
dish), and tostadas. With the selection of basic recipes for these favorites given below, we also present
one for Carnitas Fiesta, a festive combination of
pork, tortillas, and bright salsas. Try any of these
dishes when you want to offer a tantalizing
Mexican treat.

Quesadillas con Salsa de Chile Rojo

QUESADILLAS WITH RED CHILE PURÉE

Pictured on facing page

Preparation time: 40 minutes
Cooking time: About 10 minutes

In these pan-grilled quesadillas, tender melted
cheese provides a mellow foil for a piquant chile
sauce and fresh cilantro sprigs. Our easy method
lets you cook several quesadillas at once.

>   1 **cup Red Chile Purée (page 48)**
>   1 **cup (4 oz.)** *each* **shredded jack and Cheddar
>   cheeses**
>   **Butter or margarine**
>   8 **corn tortillas (6-inch diameter)**
>   **Fresh cilantro (coriander) sprigs (optional)**

Prepare Red Chile Purée; set aside. Combine jack
and Cheddar cheeses.

In a 10- to 12-inch frying pan, melt 2 tablespoons butter over medium heat. Lay a tortilla
in pan; when slightly warm, spread ¼ cup of the
cheese mixture over half the tortilla. With a spatula, fold other half over. Push to one side of pan
and add another tortilla. Repeat until pan is filled,
adding more butter as necessary.

Cook quesadillas, turning as needed, until
lightly browned (about 1 minute). Remove from
pan and keep warm; continue until all tortillas
are cooked.

Spoon 2 tablespoons of the purée over each
quesadilla and garnish with cilantro, if desired.
Makes 4 servings (2 quesadillas each).

*Per serving: 495 calories, 19 g protein, 35 g carbohydrates,
33 g total fat, 86 mg cholesterol, 450 mg sodium*

A bright, minty salsa accents Chiles Rellenos Picadillo (shown at bottom); above,
a thick chile purée creates the perfect foil for cheesy Quesadillas con Salsa de Chile Rojo.
Pair these Mexican favorites for a simple but zesty menu. You can assemble each
dish in steps, minimizing last-minute fuss. The recipes are on the facing page.

Chilaquiles con Chorizo

TORTILLA CASSEROLE WITH CHORIZO

Pictured on page 38

Preparation time: About 3 hours; 35 minutes if using purchased chorizo
Baking time: About 30 minutes

Legend tells us that *chilaquiles* originally meant "broken up old sombrero" in the ancient Aztec language. "Broken up old tortillas" makes more sense, because chilaquiles is a thrifty dish that uses up stale tortillas. You fry the pieces in oil, then coat them in a sauce. A casserolelike dish emerges with a hearty texture and rich corn flavor.

Frying fresh tortillas works just as well—but when you have stale ones, here's a great way to use them.

- ½ **pound Chorizo (page 39) or purchased chorizo sausages, casings removed**
- 1 **pound (2 to 3 medium-size) ripe tomatoes, cored, seeded, and coarsely chopped**
- 1 **medium-size onion, sliced**
- 2 **cloves garlic, peeled**
- 2 **serrano or jalapeño chiles, stemmed**
- ¼ **cup packed fresh cilantro (coriander) leaves**
- 8 **corn tortillas (6-inch diameter)**
  Salad oil
- ¼ **cup regular-strength chicken broth**
- ¾ **cup sour cream**
- 1 **cup (about 5 oz.) grated or crumbled cotija (page 13) or Romano cheese**

Prepare Chorizo; set aside.

In a blender or food processor, combine tomatoes, onion, garlic, chiles, and cilantro; whirl until puréed. Set aside.

Stack tortillas and cut into 8 wedges. Pour oil to a depth of ½ inch into a wide 3- to 4-quart pan over medium-high heat. When oil is hot, add tortilla wedges in batches and cook until stiff but not crispy (about 30 seconds). Drain on paper towels.

Pour off all but 1 tablespoon of the oil; crumble meat into pan and cook, stirring, over medium-high heat until browned (about 4 minutes). Pour in tomato purée and increase heat to high. Cook, scraping bottom of pan constantly to keep sauce from scorching, until hot and thickened (about 3 minutes). Add tortillas and broth. Continue to cook, stirring constantly, until tortillas are soft and excess liquid has been absorbed (about 2 more minutes).

Spread a third of the tortilla mixture in a 2-quart baking dish; top with half the sour cream and a third of the cheese. Repeat; then top with remaining tortilla mixture and cheese.

Bake, uncovered, in a 350° oven until bubbly and golden (about 30 minutes). Makes 4 to 6 servings.

Per serving: 432 calories, 15 g protein, 26 g carbohydrates, 30 g total fat, 56 mg cholesterol, 383 mg sodium

Chilaquiles con Pollo

TORTILLA CASSEROLE WITH CHICKEN

Preparation time: About 30 minutes
Baking time: 45 to 50 minutes

Unlike most *chilaquiles*, this version does not require frying the tortillas, resulting in a texture that's less chewy than usual.

- **Salsa Verde (recipe follows)**
- 4 **cups shredded cooked chicken, skinned**
- 1 **cup sour cream**
- ½ **cup whipping cream**
- 12 **corn tortillas (6-inch diameter), cut into ¼-inch-wide strips**
- 4 **cups (1 lb.) firmly packed shredded Cheddar cheese**
- ⅓ **cup grated Parmesan cheese**
- 1 **large ripe avocado, pitted, peeled, and thinly sliced**

Prepare Salsa Verde; set aside.

Place half the chicken in a 9- by 13-inch baking dish. Spread with half the salsa. Mix sour cream and whipping cream and spread half the mixture over salsa. Top with half the tortilla strips and half the Cheddar cheese. Repeat layers, using remaining chicken, salsa, cream mixture, tortilla chips, and Cheddar cheese.

Cover and bake in a 350° oven for 40 minutes. Uncover, sprinkle with Parmesan cheese, and continue baking until cheese is bubbly (5 to 10 more minutes).

Remove from oven. Let stand for 10 minutes; then arrange avocado slices on top of casserole. Cut into squares to serve. Makes 8 servings.

Salsa Verde. In a blender or food processor, combine 1 can (13 oz.) **tomatillos** and their liquid; 1 large **onion,** cut into chunks; 1 clove **garlic;** and 1 small can (4 oz.) **diced green chiles.** Whirl until smooth.

Per serving: 659 calories, 44 g protein, 26 g carbohydrates, 42 g total fat, 169 mg cholesterol, 785 mg sodium

Tostadas de Jaiba
CRAB TOSTADAS

Pictured on page 22

Preparation time: 20 to 30 minutes
Cooking time: About 10 minutes

Place a crisp flour tortilla, like an edible "plate," under beans, cheese, lettuce, and exciting toppings—and a tostada is born. This light version, popular in Tampico on the Gulf of Mexico, features crabmeat; meat or chicken can be substituted for a more traditional tostada.

> **Tomatillo Salsa (page 49) or purchased mild green salsa**
> **Salad oil**
> 4 **flour tortillas (7- to 9-inch diameter)**
> 2 **large ripe avocados**
> 2 **tablespoons lime juice**
> **Salt**
> 2 **cans (about 1 lb. *each*) black beans, heated**
> 1 **cup (4 oz.) shredded Cheddar cheese**
> 4 **cups shredded lettuce**
> 1 **pound crabmeat**
> 2 **medium-size tomatoes, sliced into half-rounds**
> ½ **cup sliced ripe olives**

Prepare Tomatillo Salsa; cover and refrigerate.

Pour oil to a depth of ½ inch into a 10- to 12-inch frying pan over medium-high heat. When oil is hot, add tortillas, one at a time, and cook, turning once, until crisp and golden brown (about 30 seconds per side). Drain on paper towels.

Pit, peel, and slice avocados. Add lime juice and mash with a fork. Season to taste with salt.

Evenly spread each tortilla with beans; then sprinkle with cheese, lettuce, and crabmeat. Garnish with avocado mixture, tomatoes, and olives. Offer salsa to spoon on individual servings. Makes 4 servings.

Per serving: 867 calories, 51 g protein, 77 g carbohydrates, 42 g total fat, 143 mg cholesterol, 1,723 mg sodium

TOSTADAS WITH MEAT

Prepare as directed for **Crab Tostadas** (above), substituting 1½ cups Refried Beans (page 89) or purchased refried beans for black beans and 2 cups **Carnitas** (page 39), **Ground Beef Filling** (page 21), or shredded **cooked chicken** for crabmeat. Offer as additional garnishes 2 **hard-cooked eggs,** sliced; ½ cup **sour cream;** 4 **green onions** (including tops), thinly sliced; and crumbled **queso fresco** (page 13). Makes 4 servings.

Per serving: 1,004 calories, 43 g protein, 70 g carbohydrates, 64 g total fat, 240 mg cholesterol, 830 mg sodium

Carnitas Fiesta
PORK & TORTILLA PLATTERS

Pictured on cover

Preparation time: About 1 hour
Cooking time: 4 to 5 hours

At your next party, show off this colorful dish of tender braised pork, beans, warm tortillas, and lively salsas. The salsas can be prepared in advance to cut down on last-minute work.

Arrange each element separately on the table and let your guests build their own carnitas platters. For a complete menu, see page 8.

> **Red Chile Purée (page 48)**
> **Tomatillo Salsa (page 49)**
> **Salsa Fresca (page 48)**
> **Carnitas (page 39)**
> **Frijoles Borrachos (page 90)**
> 20 **flour tortillas (7- to 9-inch diameter)**
> 2 **cups (about 8 oz.) grated or crumbled queso fresco (page 13) or mild feta cheese**

Prepare Red Chile Purée, Tomatillo Salsa, and Salsa Fresca. If made ahead, cover and refrigerate. Bring to room temperature before serving.

Prepare Carnitas and Frijoles Borrachos. Keep meat and beans warm.

Divide tortillas into 2 stacks, wrap in foil, and heat in a 350° oven until warm (15 minutes).

To assemble, spoon about ½ cup of the meat and about ¼ cup of the beans into each tortilla; roll up. Place 2 filled tortillas, seam sides down, on each dinner plate. Spoon chile purée along one side of tortillas and tomatillo salsa along other side. Spoon salsa fresca in a band across center of tortillas; sprinkle with cheese. Makes 10 servings.

Per serving: 815 calories, 49 g protein, 95 g carbohydrates, 27 g total fat, 110 mg cholesterol, 1,449 mg sodium

*What could be more satisfying than a Mexican casserole? Chilaquiles con Chorizo
(recipe on page 36), in which tortillas, spicy sausages, and tomato
sauce bake with cheese, offers delicious proof. Balance it with Ensalada de Merida
(recipe on page 56), a cool medley of citrus fruits, apples, and cilantro.*

MEAT FILLINGS

One of the most appetizing aspects of many Mexican dishes is their versatility—you can create exciting new flavors just by varying the filling. Use any of the following fillings for tacos, flautas, burritos, chimichangas, tamales, or enchiladas.

Carnitas

BRAISED PORK

Preparation time: About 10 minutes
Cooking time: 3½ to 4½ hours

Tender pork is shredded or torn into chunks and appropriately called *carnitas*, or "little meats."

- **1 bone-in pork shoulder or butt (4 to 5 lbs.)**
  About 4 cups regular-strength chicken broth
- **1 large onion, quartered**
- **1 tablespoon *each* coriander seeds and cumin seeds**
- **1 teaspoon dry oregano leaves**
- **3 canned chipotle chiles in adobo sauce (optional)**
- **2 bay leaves**

Place pork, broth, onion, coriander, cumin, oregano, chiles, if desired, and bay leaves in a 5- to 6-quart pan. Add enough water just to cover meat. Cover pan and bring to a boil; reduce heat and simmer until meat pulls apart easily with a fork (3 to 4 hours).

Lift out meat (reserve broth for other uses, if desired). Discard fat. Place pork in a large roasting pan and bake, uncovered, in a 450° oven until sizzling and browned (about 20 minutes). Pull off chunks of meat and shred with 2 forks, discarding fat. Makes 6 to 8 servings.

Per serving: 262 calories, 32 g protein, 2 g carbohydrates, 13 g total fat, 106 mg cholesterol, 374 mg sodium

Pollo Deshebrado

SHREDDED CHICKEN

Preparation time: About 15 minutes
Cooking time: About 15 minutes

This recipe injects Latin spirit into leftover chicken or turkey. Wrapped in a tortilla, it's sure to become a favorite last-minute entrée.

- **⅔ cup Red Chile Sauce (page 24) or canned enchilada sauce**
- **1½ tablespoons salad oil**
- **1 medium-size onion, chopped**
- **2 cups finely shredded cooked chicken or turkey**
- **1 pickled jalapeño or other small chile, stemmed and minced**
- **2 tablespoons chopped ripe olives (optional)**

Prepare Red Chile Sauce; set aside.

Heat oil in a wide frying pan over medium heat. When oil is hot, add onion and cook, stirring, until soft (about 5 minutes). Stir in chicken, chile, olives, and sauce. Reduce heat and simmer, uncovered, stirring occasionally, for 10 minutes. Makes 6 to 8 servings (about 3 cups).

Per serving: 116 calories, 11 g protein, 3 g carbohydrates, 7 g total fat, 31 mg cholesterol, 94 mg sodium

Chorizo

MEXICAN SAUSAGE

Preparation time: About 3¼ hours, including time to soak chiles
Chilling time: At least 2 hours
Cooking time: About 7 minutes

Deliciously spicy as a filling, chorizo can also be shaped into sausage patties or links.

- **5 or 6 (about 3 oz. *total*) dried New Mexico chiles**
- **½ cup red wine vinegar**
- **½ medium-size onion, quartered**
- **2¼ pounds ground pork**
- **4 cloves garlic, minced or pressed**
- **1½ teaspoons salt**
- **2½ teaspoons dry oregano leaves**
- **½ teaspoon *each* ground cumin and ground red pepper (cayenne)**

Soak chiles in vinegar until soft (3 hours). Remove stems and seeds. Place chiles, vinegar, and onion in a blender; whirl until smooth.

In a large bowl, combine chile purée, pork, garlic, salt, oregano, cumin, and ground red pepper; mix well. Cover and refrigerate for at least 2 hours or until next day.

Crumble desired amount of pork mixture into a frying pan over medium-high heat. Cook, stirring, until browned (about 7 minutes). Drain off any fat. Or shape mixture into patties or links and cook until no longer pink inside (about 10 minutes). Makes 8 to 10 servings (2¼ pounds).

Per serving: 255 calories, 16 g protein, 5 g carbohydrates, 19 g total fat, 70 mg cholesterol, 380 mg sodium

Appetizers & Antojitos

*A*ntojitos, or "little whims," are one of the joyful discoveries of Mexican food. Mexicans partake of these simple snacks whenever the urge strikes, no matter what time of day.

*W*ith this chapter, you can sample classic Mexican antojitos and other appetizers. Some are light—a platter of jicama and fruit brightened with chili powder, or an oil-free tortilla chip for dipping. Some, like *chalupas* (masa "boats" laden with beans and garnishes), are almost a meal in themselves.

*E*njoy antojitos as appetizers before lunch or dinner, as midday snacks, or whenever you have a whim for one.

Nachos

TORTILLA CHIPS WITH MELTED CHEESE

Preparation time: 10 to 20 minutes
Baking time: About 10 minutes

Here are nachos the way they're made in Mexico: simple, hot, and cheesy. For a more American version, top with Guacamole (page 44) as well.

    **About 7 cups (8 oz.) Fried Tortilla Chips,
    homemade (recipe at right) or purchased**
6 **ounces (1½ cups *each*) shredded Cheddar and
   jack cheeses**
1 **large can (7 oz.) diced green chiles**
   Sour cream and sliced ripe olives (optional)

Prepare Fried Tortilla Chips. Spread a third of the chips in a 4-quart baking dish. Top with a third of the cheese; then add a third of the chiles. Repeat 2 more times.

Bake in a 400° oven until cheese is melted (about 10 minutes). Garnish with several spoonfuls of sour cream and olives, if desired. Serve at once. Makes 6 to 8 servings.

*Per serving: 340 calories, 13 g protein, 20 g carbohydrates,
23 g total fat, 41 mg cholesterol, 399 mg sodium*

Cacahuates

SPICED PEANUTS

Preparation time: 10 minutes, plus 1 day standing time
Cooking time: About 6 minutes

To intensify the flavors, make these irresistible peanuts from Oaxaca a day ahead of munching. Serve with ice cold beer.

20 **small dried whole red chiles**
 4 **cloves garlic, minced or pressed**
 2 **tablespoons olive oil**
 2 **pounds salted peanuts**
 1 **teaspoon coarse or kosher salt**
 1 **teaspoon chili powder**

In a wide frying pan, combine chiles, garlic, and oil. Cook over medium heat, stirring constantly, for 1 minute.

Add peanuts. Stir over medium heat until slightly browned (about 5 minutes).

Sprinkle with salt and chili powder. Mix well.

Let cool; then store in an airtight container for at least 1 day or for up to 2 weeks. Makes about 20 servings (7 cups).

*Per serving: 278 calories, 12 g protein, 9 g carbohydrates,
24 g total fat, 0 mg cholesterol, 272 mg sodium*

Totopos

FRIED TORTILLA CHIPS

Preparation time: About 5 minutes
Cooking time: About 15 minutes

This is the all-purpose chip for dunking into salsas, dips, and Guacamole (page 44). To avoid extra fat, prepare the water-crisped variation instead of frying the tortilla chips in oil.

12 **corn tortillas (6-inch diameter)**
    Salad oil
    Salt (optional)

Stack tortillas and cut into 6 or 8 wedges.

Pour oil to a depth of 1 inch into a wide frying pan and heat to 350°F on a deep-frying thermometer. When oil is hot, add tortilla wedges in batches and cook, turning occasionally with a slotted spoon, until golden brown and crisp (30 to 60 seconds). Drain on paper towels and sprinkle with salt, if desired. If made ahead, store in an airtight container for up to 2 days. Makes about 2 quarts.

*Per cup: 193 calories, 3 g protein, 21 g carbohydrates,
11 g total fat, 0 mg cholesterol, 2 mg sodium*

WATER-CRISPED TORTILLA CHIPS

One at a time, immerse 12 **corn tortillas** (6-inch diameter) in water. Drain briefly; lay flat and sprinkle one side with **salt,** if desired. Stack and cut into 6 or 8 wedges. Arrange in a single layer (do not overlap) on a 10- by 15-inch baking sheet. Bake in a 500° oven for 4 minutes. Turn with tongs and continue baking until golden brown and crisp (3 more minutes). Repeat until all chips are cooked. If made ahead, store in an airtight container for up to 2 weeks. Makes about 2 quarts.

*Per cup: 103 calories, 3 g protein, 21 g carbohydrates, 1 g total
fat, 0 mg cholesterol, 2 mg sodium*

Chalupas

FILLED MASA BOATS

Preparation time: About 1 hour
Cooking time: 10 to 20 minutes

Chalupas, or "canoes" of fried masa, carry cargoes of hot and cold condiments. They're popular street snacks in Mexico.

  6 **cups dehydrated masa flour (corn tortilla flour)**
  1 **teaspoon salt**
  ⅔ **cup solid vegetable shortening or lard, at room temperature**
  3 **cups cold water**
      Salad oil
      Salsa Fresca, homemade (page 48) or purchased
  4 **cans (15 oz. *each*) refried beans or black beans, drained**
  2 **large ripe avocados, pitted, peeled, and thinly sliced**
  2 **cups (8 oz.) grated or crumbled cotija (page 13) or Parmesan cheese**
  4 **to 6 limes, quartered (optional)**

In a bowl, combine masa, salt, and vegetable shortening. Rub mixture with your fingers until fine crumbs form. Add water and stir until dough holds together; then work with your hands until evenly moistened.

Divide dough into 27 equal portions (keep covered with plastic wrap to prevent drying out). Use your thumbs to press each portion into an oval about 4 inches long and 2½ inches wide. Pinch up edges to form a ½-inch rim. Keep shaped shells covered with a damp towel.

Pour oil to a depth of ½ inch into a wide frying pan and heat to 375°F on a deep-frying thermometer. When oil is hot, place 3 or 4 shells, cupped sides down, in hot oil and cook until rims are browned. Using a slotted spoon, turn shells over and continue to cook until bases are browned (about 2 minutes total); if insides of shells do not brown, spoon hot oil into cupped area. Invert onto paper towels and repeat for remaining shells. (At this point, you may let cool completely, cover, and store at room temperature for up to a day. Reheat on baking sheets in a 350° oven until hot, about 20 minutes.)

Prepare Salsa Fresca; set aside.

In a 4- to 6-quart pan, cook beans over medium heat, stirring often, until hot (about 10 minutes); keep warm.

To serve, fill each shell with 2 tablespoons of the beans, 2 or 3 avocado slices, and 1 tablespoon each of the salsa and cheese. Squeeze lime over each chalupa, if desired. Makes 9 to 12 servings.

Per serving: 326 calories, 10 g protein, 33 g carbohydrates, 18 g total fat, 7 mg cholesterol, 510 mg sodium

Queso al Horno

GRILLED CHEESE APPETIZER

Pictured on facing page

Preparation time: About 20 minutes
Cooking time: About 20 minutes

The perfect outdoor party idea: you use the barbecue both to cook and serve this bubbly cheese appetizer.

      Fried Tortilla Chips, homemade (page 41) or purchased
  1½ **tablespoons olive oil**
  1 **large onion, chopped**
  2 **large tomatoes, seeded and coarsely chopped**
  ¼ **teaspoon ground cinnamon**
  4 **to 6 fresh jalapeño chiles or other small hot chiles, stemmed and chopped**
      Salt (optional)
  2 **pounds Münster, jack, or fontina cheese**
  1 **cup small cooked shrimp**
  1 **fresh whole jalapeño chile**

Prepare Fried Tortilla Chips; set aside.

Heat oil in a wide frying pan over medium-high heat. When oil is hot, add onion and cook, stirring, until soft (about 10 minutes). Add tomatoes and cinnamon. Increase heat to high and cook, stirring, for 1 minute. Add chopped chiles and, if desired, season to taste with salt. Set aside.

Meanwhile, trim rind from cheese and cut into ¼-inch-thick slices. Arrange in an 8- to 10-inch heatproof baking dish at least 1½ inches deep, overlapping slices to cover bottom. (At this point, you may cover and let stand for up to 4 hours at room temperature; cover and refrigerate tomato mixture separately.)

Just before serving, spread tomato mixture in a 6-inch circle on top of cheese; sprinkle with shrimp. Garnish with whole chile.

Place dish on a grill 4 to 6 inches above a bed of medium-hot coals that have been pushed to one side of barbecue. As cheese melts, move dish to cooler part of barbecue. Offer chips to scoop up mixture. Makes 12 servings.

Per serving: 320 calories, 21 g protein, 3 g carbohydrates, 25 g total fat, 89 mg cholesterol, 435 mg sodium

For carefree outdoor entertaining right off the grill, serve your guests bubbly Queso al Horno (recipe on facing page). Fresh tomatoes, lively chiles, tender pink shrimp, and golden cheese combine in this substantial starter to scoop up with tortilla chips. Accompany with Margaritas (recipe on page 124).

Chile con Queso
MELTED CHEESE DIP

Preparation time: 15 to 25 minutes
Cooking time: About 10 minutes

Try dunking red and green bell pepper strips, as well as tortilla chips, in Mexico's answer to cheese fondue. Mexican cooks use Chihuahua cheese in chile con queso, but Longhorn Cheddar cheese is also delicious.

　　Fried Tortilla Chips, homemade (page 41) or purchased
　2　tablespoons salad oil
　1　medium-size onion, finely chopped
　1　small can (4 oz.) diced green chiles
　⅓　cup heavy cream
　1　cup (4 oz.) shredded Longhorn Cheddar or Chihuahua cheese (page 13)
　6　medium-size green or red bell peppers, seeded and cut into ½-inch-wide strips

Prepare Fried Tortilla Chips; set aside.

　　In a 3- to 4-quart pan, combine oil and onion. Cook, stirring, over medium heat until onion is soft (about 7 minutes). Add chiles and cream. Cook, stirring, until hot. Reduce heat to low and add cheese, stirring until melted.

　　Pour into a chafing or fondue dish over a low flame or into a dish on an electric warming tray (low setting). Offer with bell pepper strips and chips. Makes 6 to 8 servings (2 cups).

Per serving: 142 calories, 4 g protein, 5 g carbohydrates, 12 g total fat, 28 mg cholesterol, 180 mg sodium

Guacamole
AVOCADO DIP

Preparation time: 10 to 20 minutes

Both a dip and a sauce, *guacamole* literally means "avocado concoction." Whatever its use, it should be prepared with ripe, buttery avocados and a touch of heat from chiles.

　　Fried Tortilla Chips, homemade (page 41) or purchased, or Water-crisped Tortilla Chips (page 41)
　2　large ripe avocados
　2　to 3 tablespoons lemon or lime juice
　1　clove garlic, minced or pressed
　1　to 2 tablespoons chopped fresh cilantro (coriander)

　2　to 4 canned green chiles, rinsed, seeded, and chopped
　1　medium-size tomato, peeled, seeded, and chopped
　　Minced jalapeño or serrano chiles (optional)
　　Salt
　　Fresh cilantro (coriander) sprigs

Prepare Fried Tortilla Chips; set aside.

　　Pit avocados and scoop out pulp. Mash pulp coarsely with a fork; blend in lemon juice, garlic, chopped cilantro, green chiles, and tomato. If desired, add jalapeño chiles to taste. Season to taste with salt. Spoon into a serving bowl and garnish with cilantro sprigs. Serve with chips. Makes about 1⅔ cups.

Per tablespoon: 33 calories, .43 g protein, 2 g carbohydrates, 3 g total fat, 0 mg cholesterol, 10 mg sodium

Antojito de Frijoles Negros
BLACK BEAN DIP

Preparation time: 15 minutes
Cooking time: 8 to 10 minutes

Layer canned black beans with vegetables and spices for a quick and easy variation of refried bean dip. For dippers, tuck fresh jicama slices or tortilla chips around beans.

　　Guacamole (recipe at left)
　6　slices bacon, coarsely chopped
　1　small onion, chopped
　½　teaspoon chili powder
　1　can (15 oz.) black beans, drained (reserve ⅓ cup of the liquid)
　1　cup (4 oz.) shredded jack cheese
　1　*each* small red and yellow bell peppers (or 2 of either), stemmed, seeded, and chopped
　¼　cup thinly sliced green onions (including tops)
　　Sour cream
　　Fresh cilantro (coriander) sprigs
　1　jicama, peeled and cut into 2-inch-wide sticks, or Fried Tortilla Chips, homemade (page 41) or purchased

Prepare Guacamole; set aside.

　　In an 8- to 10-inch frying pan, combine bacon, onion, and chili powder. Cook over medium heat, stirring occasionally, until bacon is crisp (8 to 10 minutes). Drain and discard fat. Let cool.

In a large bowl, coarsely mash beans. Stir in reserved liquid and add bacon mixture. Spread into an 8-inch round on a large platter; top with guacamole. Sprinkle with cheese; add bell peppers and green onions. Garnish with a spoonful of sour cream and cilantro sprigs. Tuck jicama slices around edge. Makes 6 to 8 servings.

Per serving: 260 calories, 10 g protein, 20 g carbohydrates, 17 g fat, 16 mg cholesterol, 480 mg sodium

Machaca Picante

SPICY MEXICAN JERKY

Preparation time: About 20 minutes
Marinating time: At least 6 hours
Cooking time: 5 to 6 hours

In Mexican markets, strips of lime and salt-seasoned beef dry in the open air. Our version involves oven-drying and a more complex blend of spices.

Partially freeze the meat before seasoning to make slicing easier. Cut with the grain if you like chewy jerky, across the grain for a more tender, but brittle, texture.

- 1 to 1½ pounds boneless beef top round, partially frozen
- 2 tablespoons *each* water and Worcestershire
- 1 teaspoon salt
- 2 cloves garlic, minced or pressed
- ⅛ teaspoon ground red pepper (cayenne)
- 1 teaspoon ground cumin
- 1½ teaspoons chili powder

Trim and discard fat from meat. Slice meat with or across grain in strips ⅛ inch thick and as long as possible.

In a bowl, combine water, Worcestershire, salt, garlic, ground red pepper, cumin, and chili powder. Stir until well blended. Add meat strips and mix thoroughly. Cover and marinate for at least 6 hours or until next day.

Shake off any excess liquid. Arrange strips of meat close together, but not overlapping, on racks set in 2 rimmed, foil-lined 9- by 13-inch baking pans.

Dry meat in a 200° oven until meat has turned dark brown and feels dry (5 to 6 hours). Pat off any beads of oil. Let cool; then remove from racks and store in airtight containers. Makes 5 to 6 ounces.

Per ounce: 103 calories, 16 g protein, 2 g carbohydrates, 3 g total fat, 39 mg cholesterol, 465 mg sodium

Flores de Calabacitas Rellenas

CHEESE-STUFFED SQUASH BLOSSOMS

Preparation time: About 30 minutes
Cooking time: 15 to 20 minutes

Bright yellow squash blossoms are prized morsels on a Mexican menu. With a zesty chile-cheese stuffing, each bloom becomes an elegant and savory appetizer.

Look for squash blossoms during the summer months in specialty produce stores and Latin or Mediterranean markets. Your best source, however, is the garden—a squash patch is replete with blossoms as delicious to eat as the vegetable itself. Because they wither quickly, squash blossoms should be used within a day of purchasing or picking.

- 15 to 20 squash blossoms (*each* about 3 inches from base to tip)
- 1 small package (3 oz.) cream cheese, softened
- 1 tablespoon milk
- ⅓ cup grated Parmesan cheese
  Dash of pepper
- 1½ tablespoons canned diced green chiles
  All-purpose flour
- 2 eggs
- 1 tablespoon water
  Salad oil

Rinse blossoms with cool water; shake off excess. Pat dry gently with paper towels. Trim off stems. Remove stamens, if necessary, to enlarge cavity before stuffing. Set aside.

In a bowl, blend cream cheese, milk, Parmesan cheese, pepper, and chiles. Spoon about 1 teaspoon of the filling into each blossom; twist tips to close. Roll blossoms in flour to coat lightly; set aside.

Beat eggs and water. Pour oil to a depth of ¼ inch into a wide frying pan over medium-high heat. When oil is hot, use a fork to dip one blossom at a time into egg mixture and place in pan. Cook 2 or 3 at a time, turning as needed, until golden brown (about 2 minutes total). Drain on paper towels; keep warm until all are cooked. Makes 15 to 20 appetizers.

Per appetizer: 59 calories, 2 g protein, 2 g carbohydrates, 5 g total fat, 33 mg cholesterol, 48 mg sodium

A mosaic of colors and textures, Jicama y Ensalada de Frutas (recipe on facing page) is showered with chili powder for zesty flavor. Watermelon, honeydew, papaya, oranges, and jicama are cut into bite-size shapes for this popular Mexican antojito; lime juice squeezed over all keeps it fresh.

Empanadas

MEAT-FILLED TURNOVERS

Pictured on page 59

Preparation time: About 1 hour
Cooking time: About 20 minutes

Traditionally, these turnovers enclose a sweet-savory meat and raisin combination called *picadillo* and are either fried or baked. You can also make bite-size empanaditas to serve as hors d'oeuvres.

> Cornmeal Pastry (recipe follows)
> 1 teaspoon butter or margarine
> ½ pound *each* ground beef and ground pork, or 1 pound ground beef
> 1 large clove garlic, minced or pressed
> ½ cup *each* tomato purée and seedless raisins
> ¼ cup dry sherry
> 2 teaspoons ground cinnamon
> ½ teaspoon ground cloves
> 2 tablespoons vinegar
> 1 tablespoon sugar
> ¾ cup slivered almonds
> Salt
> Salad oil (optional)

Prepare Cornmeal Pastry and chill as directed.

In a wide frying pan, melt butter over medium heat; crumble meat into pan and cook, stirring often, until no longer pink. Drain off excess fat. Stir in garlic, tomato purée, raisins, sherry, cinnamon, cloves, vinegar, and sugar. Cook, uncovered, until most of the liquid has evaporated (about 20 minutes). Stir in almonds; season to taste with salt and let cool.

On a floured board, roll out pastry ⅛ inch thick. Cut into 3-inch rounds for small turnovers or 5-inch rounds for large turnovers. Spoon equal amounts of the meat filling onto a side of each pastry round. Moisten edges with water, fold over, and press together with a fork.

To fry, pour oil to a depth of 1½ inches into a wide frying pan and heat to 375°F on a deep-frying thermometer. When oil is hot, add turnovers in batches and cook until golden brown on both sides (about 2 minutes total). Drain on paper towels.

To bake, arrange on a large baking sheet and place in a 400° oven for 15 to 20 minutes. Makes 40 small or 20 large empanadas.

Cornmeal Pastry. In a large bowl, combine 2 cups **all-purpose flour,** 1 cup **yellow cornmeal,** 1 tablespoon **baking powder,** and ½ teaspoon **salt.** Using a pastry blender or 2 knives, cut in 4 tablespoons cold **butter** or margarine until mixture resembles coarse meal. Beat together 1 **egg** and ¾ cup **milk;** add to flour mixture, stirring with a fork until mixture holds together (add 1 more tablespoon milk, if necessary).

Gather dough into a ball and knead slightly; wrap in plastic wrap and chill for up to an hour.

Per small empanada (baked): 110 calories, 4 g protein, 11 g carbohydrates, 6 g total fat, 20 mg cholesterol, 96 mg sodium

Jicama y Ensalada de Frutas

JICAMA & FRESH FRUIT PLATTER

Pictured on facing page

Preparation time: 30 minutes

For festive color and flavor contrast in a light hors d'oeuvre, arrange fresh fruits with crunchy jicama, a Mexican root vegetable available in most supermarkets. Sprinkle with spicy chili powder to add Latin flair.

> 1 medium-size jicama
> Fresh Fruit (suggestions follow)
> ⅔ cup lime juice
> 1 teaspoon salt
> 1 tablespoon chili powder

With a small, sharp knife, trim off and discard ends of jicama, peel, and rinse. Cut jicama in half; then slice each half thinly. Coat jicama and fruit well with lime juice; then group each element separately on a platter.

Combine salt and chili powder; sprinkle over jicama and fruit. Makes 8 to 10 servings.

Fresh Fruit. Choose from the following, using a total of 5 pounds fruit: **Honeydew, cantaloupe, or watermelon,** rind removed and fruit cut into chunks or slices; **papaya,** peeled, seeded, and sliced crosswise; **mango,** peeled and cut off pit in large cubes; **orange,** peeled and separated into sections, white membrane discarded; **kiwi fruit,** peeled and sliced crosswise; and **green apple,** cored and sliced.

Per serving: 100 calories, 2 g protein, 25 g carbohydrates, 1 g total fat, 0 mg cholesterol, 237 mg sodium

A Salsa for Every Taste

What gives Mexican food its irresistible Latin zing? Salsas, of course—those spicy condiments that appear at every Mexican table. Here are a variety of salsas, including one to suit every palate, from shy to bold.

Salsas are made both raw, or *cruda,* and cooked. Use tangy fresh salsas crudas for dipping chips or garnishing tacos and burritos. Spoon the smooth, cooked salsas over eggs, enchiladas, and roasted meats, or serve as a dip for cold seafood.

In endless ways, the salsas that follow will give an extra punch to snacks and meals.

Cilantro-Lime Salsa

Cool and refreshing, this salsa is delicious with shellfish and eggs, or spooned over avocados.

    1 small onion, finely chopped
    1 cup chopped fresh cilantro (coriander)
    ½ cup *each* chopped parsley and salad oil
    6 tablespoons lime juice
    3 tablespoons distilled white vinegar
    2 cloves garlic, minced or pressed
    1 jalapeño or other small hot chile, stemmed, seeded, and minced

Mix onion, cilantro, parsley, oil, lime juice, vinegar, garlic, and chile in a nonmetallic bowl. If made ahead, cover and refrigerate until next day. Makes about 2½ cups.

Per tablespoon: 26 calories, 0 g protein, .4 g carbohydrates, 3 g total fat, 0 mg cholesterol, 1 mg sodium

Red Chile Purée

Use this thick, rich salsa as an improvement on ketchup. Drizzle it on eggs, enchiladas, quesadillas, and hamburgers.

        About 9 (3 oz.) dried New Mexico or California chiles
    2 cups water
    1 small onion, cut into chunks
    2 cloves garlic

Arrange chiles on a large baking sheet and cook in a 300° oven until chiles smell toasted (about 4 minutes). Let cool slightly. Discard stems and seeds.

In a 3- to 4-quart pan, combine chiles, water, onion, and garlic; cover and bring to a boil over high heat. Reduce heat, cover, and simmer until chiles are very soft (about 30 minutes). Remove from heat and let cool slightly.

In a blender or food processor, whirl chile mixture until smooth; rub purée through a fine strainer and discard residue. If made ahead, cover and refrigerate for up to a week. Makes about 2 cups.

Per tablespoon: 9 calories, .33 g protein, 2 g carbohydrates, 1 g total fat, 0 mg cholesterol, 1 mg sodium

Salsa Fresca

Pictured on page 3

Made in a blender, this quintessential Mexican condiment has a moist consistency. For a drier, chunkier texture, make it by hand.

    2 cloves garlic
    ½ medium-size onion, quartered
    1 or 2 jalapeño or other small hot chiles, stemmed and seeded
    ¼ cup packed fresh cilantro (coriander) leaves
    1 pound firm-ripe tomatoes, seeded and coarsely chopped
    2 tablespoons salad oil
        Juice of 1 lime
        Salt and pepper (optional)

To make in a blender or food processor: Combine garlic, onion, chiles, cilantro, and tomatoes in a blender or food processor and whirl briefly just until coarsely chopped. Add oil and lime juice; whirl until mixture is finely chopped. Season to taste with salt and pepper, if desired.

To make by hand: Using a sharp knife, mince garlic, onion, and chiles. Finely chop cilantro and dice tomatoes. Combine in a nonmetallic bowl; then add oil and lime juice. Season to taste with salt and pepper, if desired.

If made ahead, cover and refrigerate for up to 2 days. Makes 2 cups.

Per tablespoon: 11 calories, .13 g protein, 1 g carbohydrates, 1 g total fat, 0 mg cholesterol, 1 mg sodium

Smoky Roasted Salsa

Pictured on page 3

Roasting the ingredients in a dry frying pan gives this spicy salsa an extraordinary flavor; a chipotle chile adds heat and smokiness. Serve with meats, sausages, and beans.

- 3 **cloves garlic, peeled**
- 1 **medium-size onion, quartered**
- 3 **large tomatoes**
- 1 **canned chipotle chile in adobo sauce**
- ¼ **cup lime juice**
- 2 **tablespoons salad oil**
- ¼ **cup packed fresh cilantro (coriander) leaves**

Place a 10- to 12-inch uncoated frying pan over high heat. Add garlic, onion, and tomatoes. Cook, turning often with tongs, until charred on all sides (about 10 minutes). Remove from pan and let cool. Cut tomatoes in half crosswise and discard seeds.

In a blender or food processor, combine vegetables, chipotle, lime juice, oil, and cilantro; whirl to desired consistency (either chunky or smooth). If made ahead, cover and refrigerate for up to 3 days. Makes 3 cups.

Per tablespoon: 9 calories, .1 g protein, 1 g carbohydrates, 1 g total fat, 0 mg cholesterol, 7 mg sodium

Mild Chile Sauce

Use this gently spiced tomato-onion sauce as an excellent condiment for seafood or in place of bottled chili sauce.

- 3½ **pounds tomatoes, cored and quartered**
- 2 **Anaheim chiles, stemmed and seeded**
- 1 **large onion, quartered**
- 1 **clove garlic**
- ¾ **cup sugar**
- 1 **tablespoon salt**
- 1½ **cups cider vinegar**
- ¾ **teaspoon *each* ground cinnamon and cloves**
- ½ **teaspoon ground ginger**

In a large blender or food processor, whirl tomatoes, chiles, onion, and garlic in batches until puréed. Pour into a 4-quart pan and stir in sugar, salt, vinegar, cinnamon, cloves, and ginger.

Cook over low heat, stirring often, until thickened and reduced to 1 quart (about 1½ hours).

Let cool. If made ahead, cover and refrigerate for up to 10 days. Makes 1 quart.

Per tablespoon: 16 calories, .23 g protein, 4 g carbohydrates, 0 g total fat, 0 mg cholesterol, 105 mg sodium

Tomatillo Salsa

Pictured on page 3

Even though tomatillos are usually softened by briefly roasting them, this still qualifies as a *salsa cruda*, or raw salsa.

- 1¼ **pounds tomatillos, husks removed**
- ⅓ **cup chopped fresh cilantro (coriander)**
- 1 **jalapeño, serrano, or other small hot chile, stemmed**
- ¾ **cup regular-strength chicken broth**
- ⅓ **cup lime juice**
  Salt (optional)

Rinse tomatillos; arrange in a single layer on a baking sheet and roast in a 500° oven until slightly singed (about 15 minutes). Let cool. In a blender or food processor, whirl tomatillos with cilantro and chile. Stir in broth and lime juice; season to taste with salt, if desired. If made ahead, cover and refrigerate for up to 2 days. Makes 3 cups.

Per tablespoon: 4 calories, .17 g protein, 1 g carbohydrates, 0 g total fat, 0 mg cholesterol, 16 mg sodium

Tropical Fruit Salsa

This colorful salsa is delicious with grilled chicken, fish, or pork.

- 1 **firm-ripe mango, peeled and diced**
- 1 **cup *each* diced fresh pineapple and diced honeydew**
- ½ **cup diced red bell pepper**
- ⅓ **cup seasoned rice wine vinegar**
- 2 **tablespoons minced fresh cilantro (coriander)**
- ½ **teaspoon crushed red pepper flakes**

In a bowl, mix mango, pineapple, honeydew, bell pepper, vinegar, cilantro, and red pepper flakes. If made ahead, cover and refrigerate for up to 2 days. Makes 3½ cups.

Per tablespoon: 6 calories, 0 g protein, 2 g carbohydrates, 0 g total fat, 0 mg cholesterol, 1 mg sodium

Seviche de Vieiras

SCALLOP SEVICHE

Pictured on facing page

Preparation time: 25 minutes
Chilling time: At least 8 hours

Why does seviche stand apart from other adventures with raw fish? The secret is marinating the seafood—scallops in this version—in lime juice until it looks and tastes as if poached.

For an elegant presentation, serve with endive spears for scooping. Or add diced melon, and seviche becomes a light salad.

    ½ pound sea or bay scallops, rinsed
    ⅓ cup lime or lemon juice
    ¼ cup diced white onion
    1 or 2 fresh jalapeño or serrano chiles, stemmed, seeded, and finely diced
    2 tablespoons salad oil
    ½ teaspoon chopped fresh oregano leaves or ⅛ teaspoon dry oregano leaves
    ½ cup chopped green, red, or yellow bell pepper
    2 teaspoons minced fresh cilantro (coriander)
       Salt
       Fresh oregano sprigs
       Lime halves or wedges
    1 large head endive, separated into leaves (optional)

If using sea scallops, cut into ½-inch pieces.

In a large nonmetal bowl, stir together scallops, lime juice, onion, chiles, oil, and chopped oregano. Cover and refrigerate, stirring occasionally, for at least 8 hours or until next day.

Stir bell pepper and cilantro into scallop mixture; season to taste with salt. Garnish with oregano sprigs; offer with lime halves and, if desired, endive leaves. Serve cold. Makes 6 servings.

Per serving: 82 calories, 7 g protein, 3 g carbohydrates, 5 g total fat, 12 mg cholesterol, 64 mg sodium

HONEYDEW & SEVICHE SALAD

Prepare as directed for **Seviche de Vieiras** (above). Before chilling mixture, cut a medium-size **honeydew** into quarters and discard seeds. Cut 3 of the sections lengthwise into ¼-inch slices; remove rind, if desired. Remove and discard rind from remaining melon quarter; dice and add to seviche. Wrap melon slices airtight and chill.

To serve, divide seviche among 4 salad plates; arrange melon slices around seviche and garnish as directed. Offer with **lime.** Omit endive. Makes 4 servings.

Per serving: 236 calories, 11 g protein, 34 g carbohydrates, 8 g total fat, 19 mg cholesterol, 129 mg sodium

Mariscos

SHELLFISH COCKTAIL

Preparation time: About 15 minutes, plus 1½ hours to prepare Mild Chile Sauce
Chilling time: At least 2 hours

Ask for *mariscos* in Mexico, and you may be served any number of different shellfish dishes. This version presents a piquant appetizer of marinated shrimp or scallops accompanied by chile sauce. Serve as a first course or part of a cold buffet.

    1½ pounds raw scallops (cut in half, if large) or medium-size shrimp, peeled and deveined, or a combination of both
     4 cups water
        Salt
        Grated peel of 1 lime
     ½ cup *each* lime juice and dry white wine
        Liquid hot pepper seasoning
        Pepper
        Mild Chile Sauce (page 49) or purchased chili sauce
        Lettuce leaves, washed and crisped (optional)

Rinse shellfish. In a 3- to 4-quart pan, bring water and 2 teaspoons salt to a rolling boil. Add shellfish; reduce heat and simmer until opaque when cut (2 to 3 minutes for scallops, about 3 minutes for shrimp). Drain.

Place shellfish in a deep bowl. In another bowl, mix lime peel, lime juice, and wine. Season to taste with hot pepper seasoning; pour sauce over shellfish. Mix well and season to taste with salt and pepper. Cover and refrigerate, stirring occasionally, for at least 2 hours or until next day.

Prepare Mild Chile Sauce.

Drain shellfish. Arrange lettuce leaves on individual plates; top with shellfish and spoon on chile sauce. Or arrange shellfish on a platter and offer chile sauce in a separate bowl. Makes 6 to 8 servings.

Per serving: 82 calories, 14 g protein, 3 g carbohydrates, 1 g total fat, 28 mg cholesterol, 275 mg sodium

*Adventurous seafood lovers will rave about colorful Seviche de Vieiras
(recipe on facing page). A lime-juice marinade firms the raw shellfish while imparting
tangy flavor; finely diced chiles add heat. Offered with beer, the oregano-garnished
dish makes an exceptionally elegant appetizer on a summer evening.*

Salads & Soups

*L*ike a fiesta in a bowl,
a Mexican salad presents a colorful array of
fresh fruit, vegetables, and other enticements.
With their simple dressings, these salads
show more pride as side dishes, first courses,
or even main-dish offerings than do their
distant lettuce-and-vinaigrette cousins.

*M*exican soups more
closely resemble their counterparts in other
cuisines. They range from simple vegetable
broths to hearty one-bowl meals. Soup is
usually a first course in Mexico; or make it a
meal by serving a stack of hot, soft tortillas
alongside.

*L*et the soups and salads
in this chapter add a taste of Mexican vitality
to both everyday menus and special occasions.

Ensalada de Tomatillos con Queso

TOMATILLO & CHEESE SALAD

Preparation time: 10 minutes

As you'll agree when you taste this salad, sometimes the best recipes are the simplest. Buy firm, smooth tomatillos and rinse off their sticky coating after removing the papery husks.

- 1 **pound tomatillos**
- ¼ **cup olive oil**
- 2 **tablespoons lime juice**
- 1 **cup (about 5 oz.) grated or crumbled cotija (page 13) or Parmesan cheese**
  Pepper

Husk and wash tomatillos. Slice thinly and arrange on a platter or 4 salad plates. Combine oil and lime juice; sprinkle over tomatillos and top with cheese. Season to taste with pepper. Makes 4 servings.

Per serving: 308 calories, 16 g protein, 6 g carbohydrates, 25 g total fat, 28 mg cholesterol, 661 mg sodium

Pico de Gallo

MEXICAN FRUIT & VEGETABLE SALAD

Preparation time: About 20 minutes

As a rooster pecks at grain, so we're meant to wend our way through a platter of *pico de gallo,* which means "rooster's beak." Whether you use your fingers or a fork, it's an unforgettable treat.

- 1 **piece pineapple (2¼ to 2½ lbs.), peeled**
- 1 **jicama (¾ lb.), peeled and rinsed**
- 2 **large carrots, peeled**
- 1 **medium-size cucumber, peeled**
- 1 **large firm-ripe papaya or mango**
  Chile Lime Juice (recipe follows)
  Fresh mint sprigs (optional)
  Salt

Cut pineapple crosswise into ¼-inch-thick slices. Cut jicama into ¼-inch slices. Cut carrots diagonally into ⅛-inch slices.

Cut cucumber diagonally into 3 pieces. With an apple corer or slender knife, cut out seeds, if desired. Then cut each cucumber section diago-

nally into ¼-inch slices. Peel papaya and cut in half lengthwise; then seed and cut crosswise into ¼-inch slices.

Group each element separately on a large platter. (At this point, you may cover and refrigerate for up to 4 hours.)

Prepare Chile Lime Juice and pour over salad. Garnish with mint. Season to taste with salt. Makes 8 to 10 servings.

Chile Lime Juice. Stem and seed a small **serrano or jalapeño chile.** In a blender, combine chile with ⅓ cup **lime juice** and ¼ cup **orange juice;** whirl until puréed.

Per serving: 66 calories, 1 g protein, 16 g carbohydrates, .39 g total fat, 0 mg cholesterol, 13 mg sodium

Berza con Cilantro

CILANTRO-CABBAGE SLAW

Preparation time: 20 minutes

Fresh cilantro and a touch of lime give this crisp slaw a Mexican flair. Offer it with Chili Pork Steaks (page 72) or enchiladas.

- **Lime and Garlic Dressing (recipe follows)**
- 1 **small head green cabbage (about 1 lb.), finely shredded**
- 1 **small onion, minced**
- 2 **tablespoons minced fresh cilantro (coriander)**
- 1 **cucumber**
  Salt and pepper

Prepare Lime and Garlic Dressing; set aside.

Mix cabbage, onion, and cilantro. Peel and seed cucumber; cut into 3-inch-long sticks. (At this point, you may cover and refrigerate cabbage mixture and cucumber separately for up to 1 day.)

Stir dressing into cabbage mixture and season to taste with salt and pepper. Serve in a bowl or on a platter; garnish with cucumber. Makes 6 to 8 servings.

Lime and Garlic Dressing. Whisk together ½ cup **salad oil,** ⅓ cup **lime juice,** and 2 cloves **garlic,** minced or pressed. If made ahead, cover and refrigerate for up to 2 days; stir before using.

Per serving: 143 calories, 1 g protein, 5 g carbohydrates, 14 g total fat, 0 mg cholesterol, 13 mg sodium

Refreshingly simple, Aguacate con Salsa de Jalapeño (recipe on facing page) presents a beautiful first course. Buttery smooth avocado, crisp cucumber, ruffled lettuce, and fresh orange slices are accented by a chile- and cumin-laced dressing. A spray of fresh cilantro adds an elegant touch.

Ensalada de Espinaca con Chiles Rojos

SPINACH SALAD WITH CRISP RED CHILES

Preparation time: 40 to 50 minutes
Chilling time: At least 30 minutes

This salad, from Mexico City, is full of exciting ingredients: crunchy greens, crisp-fried chiles, and smooth cheese. The most unusual is cactus (fresh or canned); see page 103 for a full description of how to use this versatile vegetable.

> 1 **pound fresh spinach**
> ¼ **pound watercress**
> 6 **large dried New Mexico or California chiles**
> ¼ **cup salad oil**
> 1 **pound fresh whole cactus pads or 1 jar (15 oz.)** *nopalitos,* **drained and rinsed**
> 8 **cups water**
> 1 **large red onion, thinly sliced**
> 1 **cup sliced radishes**
> 1 **pound asadero (page 13) or mozzarella cheese, cut into ½-inch cubes**
> **Cider Dressing (recipe follows)**
> 2 **large ripe avocados**

Discard tough spinach and watercress stems; wash greens separately and pat dry. Wrap in paper towels and refrigerate in plastic bags for at least 30 minutes or for up to 2 days.

With scissors, cut chiles crosswise into thin strips; discard seeds and stems. Heat oil in a wide frying pan over low heat. When oil is warm, add chiles and cook until crisp; watch closely to avoid burning (2 to 3 minutes). Remove with a slotted spoon and set aside; reserve oil for dressing.

Holding each cactus pad with a kitchen towel to protect your hands, shave off spines with a sharp knife. Trim around pad to remove thorny edge; peel pads, if desired. Cut into about ½-inch squares.

In a 3- to 4-quart pan, bring water to a boil over high heat. Add fresh cactus, reduce heat, and simmer, uncovered, until barely tender when pierced (about 5 minutes). Drain, rinse well with cold water, and drain again. (If using canned cactus, omit cooking.)

Tear spinach into bite-size pieces and place in a large salad bowl with watercress, cactus, onion, radishes, and cheese. (At this point, you may cover and refrigerate for up to 4 hours.)

Prepare Cider Dressing. Pit, peel, and slice avocados; add to salad with fried chiles. Add dressing and toss well. Makes 6 to 8 servings.

Cider Dressing. Mix reserved **oil from chiles;** ⅔ cup **cider vinegar;** 1 clove **garlic,** minced or pressed; 1 tablespoon **soy sauce;** and ¼ teaspoon **pepper** until blended.

Per serving: 390 calories, 16 g protein, 19 g carbohydrates, 31 g total fat, 44 mg cholesterol, 391 mg sodium

Aguacate con Salsa de Jalapeño

AVOCADO WITH JALAPEÑO DRESSING

Pictured on facing page

Preparation time: About 25 minutes

Yogurt cools the blaze of fresh jalapeño chiles in this sophisticated salad. Serve with Chorizo Bread (page 108) for an attractive light lunch.

> **Jalapeño Dressing (recipe follows)**
> 3 **large oranges**
> 2 **large ripe avocados**
> 4 **to 8 red leaf lettuce leaves, washed and crisped**
> 1 **small cucumber, thinly sliced**
> **Fresh cilantro (coriander) sprigs (optional)**

Prepare Jalapeño Dressing; set aside.

Cut off peel and white membrane from oranges; cut crosswise into thin slices. Cut avocados in half lengthwise; pit and peel. Fan each avocado half by slicing lengthwise at ½-inch intervals, without cutting through tapered end of fruit; then push down gently on back of avocado with flat of a knife.

Place lettuce leaves on 4 dinner plates; place an avocado fan (pit side down) on each plate. For each serving, arrange orange and cucumber slices separately around avocado. Spoon 2 to 3 table-spoons of the dressing in a band over avocado. Garnish with cilantro, if desired. Makes 4 servings.

Jalapeño Dressing. Stir together ½ cup **plain yogurt;** ¼ teaspoon crushed **cumin seeds;** 1 clove **garlic,** minced or pressed; and 2 tablespoons *each* stemmed, seeded, and minced **fresh or canned jalapeño chiles, fresh orange juice,** and chopped **fresh cilantro** (coriander). Season to taste with **salt,** if desired.

Per serving: 302 calories, 6 g protein, 32 g carbohydrates, 20 g total fat, 2 mg cholesterol, 35 mg sodium

Ensalada de Merida
MERIDA SALAD

Pictured on page 38

Preparation time: About 20 minutes

Accent spicy main dishes, such as Chilaquiles con Chorizo (page 36), with this light, tart citrus salad from the town of Merida on the Yucatan peninsula.

2 large oranges
2 tangerines
2 large pink grapefruit
2 large green-skinned apples
¼ cup lime juice
  Salt (optional)
½ cup packed fresh cilantro (coriander) leaves

Holding fruit over a bowl to catch juices, use a sharp knife to cut off peel and white membrane from oranges, tangerines, and grapefruit; separate oranges, tangerines, and grapefruit into segments. Core and thinly slice apples.

Arrange fruit in a shallow serving dish and sprinkle with lime juice and any accumulated citrus juices. Season to taste with salt, if desired. Garnish with cilantro. Makes 8 servings.

Per serving: 79 calories, 1 g protein, 20 g carbohydrates, .34 g total fat, 0 mg cholesterol, 2 mg sodium

Ensalada de Noche Buena
CHRISTMAS EVE SALAD

Pictured on page 30

Preparation time: About 35 minutes

Bejeweled with pomegranate seeds and glistening with fruits, this salad traditionally appears on Christmas Eve menus. We've included an easy method for removing the seeds from their fruit.

2 pomegranates
1 head romaine lettuce
8 cooked beets (red, golden, or a combination of both), peeled and thinly sliced
4 oranges, peeled and thinly sliced
4 unpeeled red apples, cored and thinly sliced
4 bananas, peeled and thinly sliced
1 pineapple, peeled, cored, and cut into chunks, or 1 large can (32 oz.) pineapple chunks, drained
1 lime, thinly sliced
¼ cup sugar (optional)
1 cup roasted peanuts, chopped
½ cup salad oil
¼ cup red wine vinegar

Cut crown end off pomegranates and cut fruit into quarters. Submerge in a bowl of cold water and break sections apart, separating seeds from membranes with your fingers. (Seeds will sink to bottom, while membranes and rind float to top.) Skim off and discard membranes and rind; drain seeds through a fine strainer. Pat dry and set aside.

Remove 6 large outer leaves from romaine; shred remaining lettuce. Line a large, shallow serving bowl with whole leaves; then add shredded lettuce. Arrange beets, oranges, apples, bananas, and pineapple in a decorative pattern over lettuce; garnish with lime slices. Sprinkle with sugar, if desired, pomegranate seeds, and peanuts.

Mix oil and vinegar until blended; pour over salad just before serving. Makes 8 to 10 servings.

Per serving: 355 calories, 7 g protein, 46 g carbohydrates, 19 g total fat, 0 mg cholesterol, 89 mg sodium

Ensalada a la Veracruzana
VERACRUZ-STYLE FISH SALAD

Preparation time: About 35 minutes
Chilling time: At least 2 hours

Veracruz is famous throughout Mexico for its vibrant seafood specialties. In this salad, tomatoes, garlic, capers, olives, and onions surround white fish with a chorus of local flavor.

1½ pounds skinless white-fleshed fish fillets, such as rockfish, orange roughy, or halibut
2 ripe tomatoes, cored and diced
2 cloves garlic, minced or pressed
¾ cup pimento-stuffed green olives
¼ cup drained capers
⅓ cup thinly sliced green onions (including tops)
½ cup lime juice
  Salt and pepper
4 large lettuce leaves, washed and crisped
4 lime wedges

Place fish in a single layer in a 9- by 13-inch baking dish. Cover and bake in a 400° oven until fish is just slightly translucent or wet inside when cut in thickest part (about 10 minutes per inch of thickness). Let cool; then cover and refrigerate for at least 2 hours or until next day. Lift out fish and discard pan juices; remove any bones. Break fish into bite-size chunks.

In a large bowl, mix tomatoes, garlic, olives, capers, green onions, lime juice, and fish. Season to taste with salt and pepper. Place lettuce leaves on 4 salad plates and spoon equal portions of fish mixture onto each. Garnish with lime wedges. Makes 4 servings.

Per serving: 219 calories, 33 g protein, 8 g carbohydrates, 6 g total fat, 60 mg cholesterol, 947 mg sodium

Ensalada de Frijoles Negros

BLACK BEAN SALAD

Preparation time: About 30 minutes
Cooking time: About 1½ hours

A popular basis for Mexican soups, dips, and chilis, black beans produce an excellent salad as well. To preserve color and texture, rinse the beans thoroughly after cooking.

- ½ **pound (about 1¼ cups) dried black beans, sorted of debris and rinsed**
- 2 **quarts water**
- ½ **teaspoon ground red pepper (cayenne)**
- 1 **red bell pepper, stemmed, seeded, and finely chopped**
- ½ **cup diagonally sliced green onions (including tops)**
- 2 **tablespoons red wine vinegar**
- 1 **tablespoon** *each* **lemon juice and thinly slivered lemon peel (yellow part only)**
- ¼ **cup chopped fresh cilantro (coriander)**
  Salt
  Fresh cilantro (coriander) sprigs

In a 4- to 5-quart pan, combine beans, water, and ¼ teaspoon of the ground red pepper; bring to a boil over high heat. Reduce heat, cover, and simmer until beans are tender to bite (about 1½ hours); drain. Rinse until water runs clear and beans are cool (about 3 minutes). Drain well.

In a large bowl, mix beans with bell pepper, green onions, vinegar, lemon juice, lemon peel, chopped cilantro, and remaining ¼ teaspoon ground red pepper. Season to taste with salt. If made ahead, cover and refrigerate for up to a day. Garnish with cilantro sprigs. Makes 6 to 8 servings.

Per serving: 103 calories, 6 g protein, 19 g carbohydrates, .44 g total fat, 0 mg cholesterol, 3 mg sodium

Ensalada de Calamares

MEXICAN SQUID SALAD

Preparation time: About 20 minutes

To accompany this main-event seafood salad, offer Cornbread (page 108) and chilled white wine. Ask your fishmonger for cleaned squid mantles (also called hoods); use large shrimp if squid is unavailable.

  Chile Dressing (recipe follows)
- 4 **cups water**
- 2 **pounds cleaned squid mantles, cut crosswise into 1-inch-thick rings**
- 1 **small red bell pepper, stemmed, seeded, and thinly sliced**
- ¾ **cup cooked corn kernels**
- 1 **small can (8 oz.) kidney beans, drained**
  Romaine lettuce leaves, washed and crisped

Prepare Chile Dressing; set aside.

In a 4- to 5-quart pan, bring water to a boil over high heat. Add squid and cook until opaque (about 30 seconds). Drain, rinse with cold water, and let cool.

In a bowl, mix squid, dressing, bell pepper, corn, and beans. Arrange lettuce on 4 to 6 dinner plates; spoon equal amounts of the squid mixture onto lettuce. Makes 4 to 6 servings.

Chile Dressing. Mix ½ cup **salad oil**, ⅓ cup **lemon juice**, 1½ teaspoons *each* **dry oregano leaves** and **ground cumin**, and 1 or 2 **jalapeño or serrano chiles**, stemmed, seeded, and minced until blended.

Per serving: 362 calories, 27 g protein, 18 g carbohydrates, 21 g total fat, 353 mg cholesterol, 205 mg sodium

MEXICAN SHRIMP SALAD

Prepare as directed for **Mexican Squid Salad** (above), substituting 2 pounds unshelled **large shrimp** for squid. To prepare shrimp, cut down back of shell with a small, sharp knife or scissors; peel off shell, leaving tail on, if desired. Rinse shrimp under cool running water to wash out sand vein.

In a 4- to 5-quart pan, bring enough water to cover shrimp to a boil. Add shrimp; reduce heat, cover, and simmer until opaque when cut (about 4 minutes). Drain and cool.

Per serving: 352 calories, 28 g protein, 14 g carbohydrates, 21 g total fat, 186 mg cholesterol, 320 mg sodium

Gazpacho

COLD VEGETABLE SOUP

Pictured on facing page

Preparation time: 30 minutes
Chilling time: At least 4 hours

There probably exists a gazpacho variation for every cook in Mexico. Here we offer one recipe that can be made two ways—either chunky and tomato based, or light and clear with condiments.

> 1 **large cucumber**
> 2 **large tomatoes, seeded and finely chopped**
> 1 **large red or green bell pepper, seeded and finely chopped**
> 1 **small can (2¼ oz.) sliced ripe olives, drained**
> ¼ **cup lime juice**
> 3 **cups regular-strength chicken broth**
> 1 **cup tomato juice**
> 1 **clove garlic, minced or pressed**
> ½ **cup sliced green onions (including tops)**
> 1 **tablespoon chopped fresh thyme or 1 teaspoon dry thyme leaves**
> **Liquid hot pepper seasoning**

Peel cucumber and cut in half lengthwise; scrape out and discard seeds. Finely chop cucumber.

In a large bowl, combine cucumber, tomatoes, bell pepper, olives, lime juice, broth, tomato juice, garlic, green onions, and thyme. Season to taste with hot pepper seasoning. Cover and refrigerate for at least 4 hours or until next day. Makes 6 to 8 servings.

Per serving: 52 calories, 2 g protein, 7 g carbohydrates, 3 g total fat, 0 mg cholesterol, 552 mg sodium

CLEAR GAZPACHO

Prepare **cucumbers, bell peppers, olives,** and **green onions** as directed for **Gazpacho** (above), but do not mix with other ingredients. Instead, arrange separately in small bowls along with 2 large ripe **avocados,** pitted, peeled, and chopped (sprinkle with lemon juice to prevent browning); 1 cup chopped **fresh cilantro** (coriander); and 1 cup chopped **salted almonds.**

In a large bowl, combine remaining ingredients for Gazpacho except tomato juice; increase **chicken broth** to 6 cups total. Ladle soup into glass bowls; offer vegetables and garnishes to add to each portion. Makes 6 to 8 servings.

Per serving: 261 calories, 8 g protein, 13 g carbohydrates, 22 g total fat, 0 mg cholesterol, 977 mg sodium

Gazpacho de Aguacates

AVOCADO GAZPACHO

Preparation time: 30 minutes
Chilling time: At least 2 hours
Cooking time (croutons): About 20 minutes

If you love the subtle flavor and silken texture of avocado, try this unusual version of gazpacho. Choose avocados that yield just slightly when gently pushed.

> 1 **large cucumber, peeled**
> ¼ **cup firmly packed cilantro (coriander)**
> 2 **tablespoons lime juice**
> 3 **cups regular-strength chicken broth**
> 2 **medium-size ripe avocados**
> **Chili-Garlic Croutons (recipe follows)**
> 1 **small red onion**
> **Fresh cilantro (coriander) sprigs**
> 2 **limes, cut into wedges**

Cut cucumber into chunks and place in a blender with the ¼ cup cilantro, lime juice, and 2 cups of the broth; whirl until smooth.

Pit, peel, and coarsely chop avocados. Add 1 avocado to cucumber mixture and whirl until smooth; add remaining avocado and whirl very briefly to coarsely purée, leaving some chunks. Cover and refrigerate for at least 2 hours or until next day.

Just before serving, prepare Chili-Garlic Croutons and set aside. Peel onion and cut crosswise into several thin slices; separate into rings. Mince enough of the remaining onion to make ¼ cup. Mix minced onion and remaining 1 cup broth with soup.

Pour into 6 soup bowls and garnish with onion rings, croutons, and cilantro sprigs. Offer lime wedges. Makes 6 servings.

Chili-Garlic Croutons. Cut day-old **French bread** (about half a 1-lb. loaf) into ½-inch cubes. Place in a single layer in a 10- by 15-inch baking pan and bake in a 300° oven for 15 minutes.

In a wide frying pan, melt ½ cup (¼ lb.) **butter** or margarine over medium heat. Stir in 2 cloves **garlic,** minced or pressed, and ½ teaspoon *each* **ground red pepper** (cayenne), **paprika,** and **ground cumin.** Cook, stirring, until garlic is soft (about 1 minute). Add baked croutons and mix gently until evenly coated; watch carefully to avoid burning. Remove from heat; let cool.

Per serving: 389 calories, 7 g protein, 32 g carbohydrates, 28 g total fat, 43 mg cholesterol, 889 mg sodium

Pair cool, garden-fresh Gazpacho (recipe on facing page) with
warm-from-the-oven Empanadas (recipe on page 47) for an unbeatable Mexican duo.
The light, cold soup is brimming with chunky vegetables and fresh thyme. The
empanadas enclose a savory-sweet meat filling.

Sopa de Frijoles Negros

BLACK BEAN SOUP

Preparation time: About 20 minutes, plus at least 12 hours to soak beans
Cooking time: About 2 hours

Though beans are a trademark of Mexican cooking, the black bean is especially favored in Oaxaca. Here it enriches a velvety soup, laden with ham.

- 1 pound (2½ cups) dried black beans, sorted of debris
- 10 cups regular-strength chicken broth
- 1 pound ham hocks, cracked
- 2 stalks celery, chopped
- 2 cloves garlic, minced or pressed
- 2 large onions, chopped
- ½ teaspoon pepper
- ¼ teaspoon ground allspice
- 1 small can (8 oz.) tomato sauce
- ½ cup dry red wine or 3 tablespoons lemon juice
- 1 lemon, thinly sliced
  About 2 cups sour cream

Rinse beans and place in a large bowl. Cover with cold water and soak at room temperature for at least 12 hours. Drain.

In a 5-quart pan, combine beans, broth, ham, celery, garlic, onions, pepper, and allspice. Bring to a boil over high heat; reduce heat, cover, and simmer until beans mash easily (about 2 hours).

Remove ham and set aside. Stir tomato sauce and wine into soup. In a blender or food processor, whirl soup, a portion at a time, until smooth. Return to pan.

Discard skin and bones from ham hocks and dice meat; add to soup. Reheat to a gentle boil. Garnish individual servings with lemon slices and offer with sour cream. Makes 6 to 8 servings.

Per serving: 421 calories, 21 g protein, 49 g carbohydrates, 18 g total fat, 36 mg cholesterol, 1,718 mg sodium

Sopa de Albondigas

MEATBALL SOUP

Preparation time: About 20 minutes
Cooking time: About 45 minutes

Easy to prepare and full of fresh flavors, this soup is a popular choice for the *comida* (midday meal) in Mexican homes.

- 1½ pounds lean ground beef
- ¼ cup all-purpose flour
- 2 eggs
- 6 cups regular-strength chicken broth
- 4 cups regular-strength beef broth
- 1 teaspoon dry oregano leaves
- 2 medium-size onions, chopped
- 1 large dried whole ancho or pasilla chile, stemmed, seeded, and crumbled, or 2 teaspoons ground chile powder
- 6 carrots, thinly sliced
- ¼ cup long-grain white rice
- ⅓ cup chopped fresh cilantro (coriander)
- ¾ pound spinach leaves, washed
- 2 or 3 limes, cut into wedges

In a large bowl, mix beef, flour, eggs, and ½ cup of the chicken broth. Set aside.

In an 8-quart pan, combine remaining 5½ cups chicken broth, beef broth, oregano, onions, and chile. Bring to a boil over high heat; then reduce heat to low.

Quickly shape beef mixture into 1½-inch balls, dropping them into broth as you shape them. Simmer, uncovered, skimming off any fat and foam, for 5 minutes. Add carrots, rice, and cilantro. Continue to simmer, uncovered, until carrots and rice are tender to bite (about 20 minutes).

Discard tough spinach stems; cut leaves crosswise into thin shreds. Add spinach to soup and cook for 5 more minutes. Pour into bowls and offer lime wedges. Makes 6 to 8 servings.

Per serving: 308 calories, 22 g protein, 21 g carbohydrates, 16 g total fat, 118 mg cholesterol, 1,263 mg sodium

Sopa Sonorense

SONORA-STYLE OXTAIL SOUP

Preparation time: 40 minutes, plus at least 12 hours to soak beans
Cooking time: About 4 hours

From the northern state of Sonora comes this hearty meal-in-a-bowl. Slowly simmered oxtails become succulent as they enrich the bean-filled broth.

- ½ pound (1¼ cups) dried pinto beans, sorted of debris
- 4 to 5 pounds oxtails, cut into 2-inch lengths
- 2 large onions, chopped
- 4 large cloves garlic, minced or pressed
- 4 cups *each* regular-strength beef broth and water

Salsa Fresca, homemade (page 48) or
purchased
Salt and pepper
Fresh cilantro (coriander) leaves
2 cups (8 oz.) shredded jack cheese

Rinse beans and place in a large bowl. Cover with cold water and soak at room temperature for at least 12 hours. Drain.

Arrange oxtails on a rack in a 12- by 15-inch broiler pan. Broil 4 inches from heat, turning, until well browned on all sides (about 20 minutes).

In an 8- to 10-quart pan, combine beans, onions, garlic, broth, water, and oxtails; bring to a boil over high heat. Reduce heat, cover, and simmer until beans mash easily and meat pulls away from bone (about 4 hours). If made ahead, cool, cover, and refrigerate.

Prepare Salsa Fresca. Skim and discard fat from liquid. Season to taste with salt and pepper. Offer cilantro, cheese, and salsa in separate bowls to add to individual servings. Makes 6 servings.

Per serving: 513 calories, 44 g protein, 30 g carbohydrates, 25 g total fat, 33 mg cholesterol, 891 mg sodium

Sopa de Elote
CORN SOUP

Preparation time: About 10 minutes
Cooking time: About 10 minutes

Sweet corn, mild bell peppers, and chili powder mingle in this easy-to-prepare soup.

2 tablespoons butter or margarine
1 teaspoon chili powder
1 cup *each* seeded and diced green and red bell peppers
1½ cups fresh or frozen thawed corn kernels
6 cups regular-strength chicken broth
1 cup whipping cream
¼ teaspoon salt

In a 3-quart pan, melt butter over medium heat. Add chili powder and bell peppers; cook, stirring, for 3 minutes. Add corn and broth. Bring to a boil; reduce heat and simmer, uncovered, for about 5 minutes.

Whip cream with salt until stiff. Pour soup into a tureen, add whipped cream, and stir lightly. Makes 8 to 10 servings.

Per serving: 136 calories, 3 g protein, 8 g carbohydrates, 11 g total fat, 33 mg cholesterol, 695 mg sodium

Menudo
TRIPE SOUP

Preparation time: 45 minutes
Cooking time: 6 ½ to 7 ½ hours

Mexico's answer to chicken soup may not actually cure colds. But *menudo* is legendary for alleviating the morning-after symptoms of a wild night out, which is probably why it's usually served on Sundays.

3½ pounds beef tripe, rinsed well and cut into 1-inch squares
3 to 3½ pounds beef shanks
10 cups water
2 medium-size onions, chopped
10 cloves garlic, minced or pressed
2 teaspoons ground cumin
Chile Purée (recipe follows)
3 large cans (29 oz. *each*) white or yellow hominy, drained
Salt
Garnishes (suggestions follow)

In an 8- to 10-quart pan, combine tripe, beef shanks, water, onions, garlic, and cumin. Bring to a boil over high heat; reduce heat, cover, and simmer until tripe is very tender (6 to 7 hours). Meanwhile, prepare Chile Purée; set aside.

Skim and discard fat from liquid. Lift beef shanks from pan; discard bones and fat. Cut meat into chunks and return to pan with purée and hominy. Season to taste with salt. Bring to a boil; reduce heat, cover, and simmer for 30 minutes. If made ahead, cool, cover, and refrigerate for up to 2 days; reheat before serving.

Pour soup into bowls; offer garnishes to add to individual servings. Makes 10 to 12 servings.

Chile Purée. Discard stems and seeds from 9 large **dried New Mexico or California chiles.** Place chiles in a bowl with 3¼ cups **warm water.** Let stand until softened (20 to 30 minutes). Discard all but 1¼ cups of the liquid. In a blender or food processor, purée chiles with liquid until smooth, scraping sides of container once or twice.

Garnishes. Choose from the following, arranged in separate bowls: 3 **limes** or lemons, cut into wedges; ½ cup **fresh oregano leaves;** 1 cup **fresh cilantro (coriander) sprigs;** 1 medium-size **onion,** chopped; and ¼ cup **crushed dried hot red chiles** or 5 fresh serrano or jalapeño chiles, stemmed, seeded, and thinly sliced.

Per serving: 401 calories, 43 g protein, 33 g carbohydrates, 11 g total fat, 160 mg cholesterol, 703 mg sodium

A nourishing potpourri of ham, chicken, and hominy in a lightly seasoned broth,
Pozole (recipe on facing page) is a traditional and popular soup of Mexico.
Add condiments, such as diced cream cheese, red peppers, lime wedges, green salsa,
and crunchy tortilla strips, to each bowlful, turning the soup into a satisfying meal.

Pozole

PORK & HOMINY SOUP

Pictured on facing page

Preparation time: About 45 minutes
Cooking time: About 2½ hours

This robust classic is now popular throughout Mexico and the American Southwest. Our version uses readily available canned hominy.

- 2 **large cans (49½ oz. *each*) regular-strength chicken broth**
- 3 **pounds meaty ham hocks**
- 2 **pounds chicken legs, with thighs attached**
- 1 **teaspoon dry oregano leaves**
- ½ **teaspoon cumin seeds**
- 2 **large onions, cut into chunks**
  Crisp Tortilla Strips (recipe follows)
  Tomatillo Salsa (page 49) or purchased green chile salsa
- 1 **large can (29 oz.) yellow hominy, drained**
  Garnishes (suggestions follow)

In a 6- to 8-quart pan, combine broth, ham, chicken, oregano, cumin, and onions. Bring to a boil over high heat; reduce heat, cover, and simmer until meat is tender when pierced (about 2 hours). Lift out meat and set aside. Pour broth through a wire strainer and return to pan.

When ham and chicken are cool enough to handle, discard skin, bones, and fat; tear meat into chunks and return to broth. Discard onions. (At this point, you may cover and refrigerate for up to 2 days.)

Prepare Crisp Tortilla Strips and Tomatillo Salsa. Set aside.

Skim and discard fat from liquid; bring broth to a simmer. Stir in hominy; cover and cook for 30 minutes. Serve hot; offer garnishes, salsa, and tortilla strips to add to individual servings. Makes 8 to 10 servings.

Crisp Tortilla Strips. Stack 8 to 10 **corn tortillas** (6-inch diameter) and cut into ¼-inch strips. Pour **salad oil** to a depth of 1 inch into a 3- to 4-quart pan and heat to 375°F on a deep-frying thermometer. When oil is hot, add strips, a handful at a time. Cook, stirring often, until crisp and lightly browned (about 1 minute). Lift out; drain on paper towels. Sprinkle with **salt.**

Garnishes. Choose from the following: 2 or 3 **limes,** cut into wedges; 2 small packages (3 oz. *each*) **cream cheese,** diced; 2 cups shredded **iceberg** lettuce; 1 to 1½ cups thinly sliced **green onions** (including tops); and 2 large **red bell peppers,** seeded and cut into slivers.

Per serving: 524 calories, 32 g protein, 39 g carbohydrates, 27 g total fat, 107 mg cholesterol, 2,715 mg sodium

Sopa de Pollo con Tortillas

CHICKEN SOUP WITH TORTILLA STRIPS

Preparation time: About 25 minutes
Cooking time: About 1 hour and 10 minutes

A delicate accent of hot pepper, cumin, and cilantro contrasts with this creamy chicken soup. Fried tortilla strips, to eat alongside or crumble directly into each bowl, add crunch.

- **3½- to 4-pound frying chicken**
- 7 **cups water**
- 3 **small onions, cut into quarters**
  Flaky Tortilla Strips (recipe follows)
- 3 **medium-size tomatoes, cut into wedges**
- ½ **teaspoon *each* crushed dried hot red pepper and ground cumin**
- 2 **cups (1 pt.) whipping cream**
- ½ **cup fresh cilantro (coriander) sprigs**

Rinse chicken; discard fat. In a 6- to 8-quart pan, combine chicken, water, and onions. Cover and bring to a boil over high heat; reduce heat to medium and simmer until meat pulls away easily from bones (about 1 hour). Lift out chicken and let cool.

When cool enough to handle, shred meat and set aside. Discard skin and bones. Boil broth, uncovered, until reduced to about 4 cups. Pour through a wire strainer and set aside; reserve onions. Prepare Flaky Tortilla Strips.

Return onions to pan with tomatoes, hot red pepper, and cumin. Cook over medium heat, stirring, until tomatoes mash easily (about 10 minutes). Add broth, cream, and chicken; bring to a gentle boil. Pour into individual bowls and garnish with cilantro. Offer tortilla strips to eat alongside or crumble into bowls. Makes 6 servings.

Flaky Tortilla Strips. Prepare as directed for **Crisp Tortilla Strips** (at left), using 8 **flour tortillas** (7- to 9-inch diameter) instead of corn tortillas.

Per serving: 661 calories, 34 g protein, 38 g carbohydrates, 41 g total fat, 177 mg cholesterol, 409 mg sodium

Meat, Poultry & Seafood

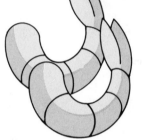

From land, sky, and sea come the succulent temptations presented in this chapter. Although most of these dishes are not well known outside of Mexico, they qualify as some of the most inspired examples of its culinary art.

From the Yucatan peninsula come subtle seasonings and unique cooking styles, such as wrapping pork in banana leaves. Northern Mexico contributes its robust tradition of grilling. And we can thank the town of Puebla for its baroque *mole* sauce for poultry. From the countless miles of coastline come seafood dishes bursting with fresh flavor.

In your next menu, introduce a sample of Mexico's artistry with meat, poultry, and seafood. It's all here.

Carne Asada
GRILLED SKIRT STEAK

Preparation time: 10 minutes
Marinating time: At least 4 hours
Grilling time: About 10 minutes

Carne asada is simplicity itself: just tender marinated skirt steaks, grilled to perfection. In northern Mexico, the sliced meat is sometimes rolled into warm flour tortillas and eaten with salsa, a precursor to the popular fajita.

Skirt steaks may require ordering ahead; flank steak is a delicious substitute, but it needs longer marinating, preferably overnight. Ask your butcher to trim excess fat, but not to roll or tenderize the meat.

⅓ cup *each* wine vinegar and olive oil
1 teaspoon dry oregano leaves
½ teaspoon coarsely ground pepper
3 to 3½ pounds skirt or flank steak
Salsa Fresca, homemade (page 48) or purchased (optional)
Flour tortillas (optional)

Combine vinegar, oil, oregano, and pepper. Place meat in a 9- by 13-inch baking dish and pour in marinade; turn to coat well. Cover and refrigerate for at least 4 hours or until next day, turning meat occasionally. Prepare Salsa Fresca, if desired.

Place meat on a grill 4 or 5 inches above a solid bed of medium-hot coals. Cook until meat is done to your liking (about 5 minutes on each side for rare; 6 minutes for flank steak). Slice diagonally across grain and serve with salsa and tortillas, if desired. Makes 6 to 8 servings.

Per serving: 366 calories, 32 g protein, .28 g carbohydrates, 25 g total fat, 91 mg cholesterol, 106 mg sodium

Bistec Ranchero
RANCH-STYLE STEAK

Preparation time: About 5 minutes
Grilling time: About 20 minutes

On the cattle ranches of northern Mexico, plain grilled meats are a delicacy. For a lively flavor, finish the steaks with a dousing of orange juice.

About 3 pounds top round steak, cut 2 inches thick
Freshly ground pepper
1 large orange

Trim off all fat from steak and make diagonal cuts about ⅜ inch deep and 1 inch apart. Rub lightly with pepper. Grill 4 or 5 inches above a solid bed of medium-hot coals until meat is done to your liking (about 10 minutes on each side for rare).

Transfer meat to carving board. Slice orange in half and squeeze juice evenly over meat. Slice meat thinly on diagonal and moisten with accumulated juices. Makes 8 to 10 servings.

Per serving: 191 calories, 31 g protein, 1 g carbohydrates, 6 g total fat, 80 mg cholesterol, 59 mg sodium

Costilla de Res en Salsa de Chipotle
BEEF SHORT RIBS IN CHIPOTLE SAUCE

Preparation time: About 15 minutes
Baking time: About 4 hours

Chipotles, or smoked red jalapeño chiles, infuse a mellow pungency and moderate heat into these slowly simmered beef ribs.

Look for canned chipotle chiles in adobo sauce (or dried ones) in Mexican markets. Occasionally, supermarkets also carry the canned type.

4 lean beef short ribs (about 4 lbs. *total*), cracked and trimmed of visible fat
1 large onion, chopped
2 canned chipotle chiles in adobo sauce or 2 dried chipotle chiles
2½ cups regular-strength chicken broth
Salt (optional)
About 3 cups hot cooked rice

In a deep 4- to 5-quart pan, arrange ribs and onion, tucking chiles among ribs. Add 1 cup of the broth and cover tightly.

Bake in a 400° oven until meat pulls away easily from bones (about 3½ hours). Uncover and bake until meat is browned (about 15 minutes). With a slotted spoon, transfer ribs and onion to a platter and keep warm. Add remaining 1½ cups broth to pan, scraping up browned bits and mashing chiles with back of a spoon. Skim and discard fat; bring juices to a boil. If desired, season to taste with salt. Serve ribs with onion, juices, and hot rice. Makes 4 servings.

Per serving: 582 calories, 43 g protein, 45 g carbohydrates, 25 g total fat, 114 mg cholesterol, 847 mg sodium

Barbacoa
SEASONED ROAST BEEF

Preparation time: About 40 minutes
Marinating time: 2 to 3 hours
Baking time: 2½ to 3 hours

Barbacoa means "barbecue," but here it refers to oven-roasting instead of grilling. The highly seasoned roast is cooked until fork-tender.

> Chile Seasoning (recipe follows)
> 5-pound bone-in beef chuck roast or 6- to 6 ½-pound leg of lamb, boned and cut into chunks
> Salt
> 3 tablespoons white wine vinegar
> Warm Tomato Salsa (recipe follows)

Prepare Chile Seasoning; set aside. Season meat to taste with salt and sprinkle with vinegar; cover and refrigerate for 2 to 3 hours.

Drain meat and place in a 5- to 6-quart pan. Spread seasoning over meat. Cover and bake in a 350° oven until very tender when pierced (2½ to 3 hours).

About 20 minutes before serving, prepare Warm Tomato Salsa. Keep warm.

To serve, lift meat from pan and cut or tear into shreds. Offer salsa to spoon over meat. Makes 6 to 8 servings.

Chile Seasoning. Discard stems and seeds from 4 **dried New Mexico or California chiles, 2 dried ancho chiles,** and 4 **small dried hot red chiles.** Tear or break chiles into pieces. Cover with ½ cup **hot water** and let stand until soft (about 20 minutes); drain.

In a blender, combine drained chiles, 10 cloves **garlic,** 1 tablespoon **dry oregano leaves,** 2 tablespoons *each* **whole cloves** and **cumin seeds,** 1 teaspoon **cracked black pepper,** ½ teaspoon **ground cinnamon,** and ½ can (13 oz.) **tomatillos,** drained. Whirl until chiles are finely chopped.

Warm Tomato Salsa. In an 8- to 10-inch frying pan, melt 2 tablespoons **butter** or margarine over medium-high heat. Add 1 large **onion,** finely chopped, and 1 **green bell pepper,** seeded and chopped. Cook, stirring, until vegetables are soft (about 10 minutes). Add 4 large **tomatoes,** peeled, seeded, and cut into chunks, and cook until tomatoes are heated through (about 2 more minutes). Season to taste with **salt** and **pepper,** if desired.

Per serving: 700 calories, 49 g protein, 12 g carbohydrates, 51 g total fat, 179 mg cholesterol, 143 mg sodium

Chili Colorado
RED CHILI WITH MEAT

Pictured on facing page

Preparation time: About 50 minutes
Cooking time: 3 to 4 hours

Boldly seasoned with dried chiles, this chunky stew is the great granddaddy of the chili con carne that has become famous north of the border. It's prepared without beans, as is preferred in Mexico.

> 4 ounces dried New Mexico chiles
> 3 cups water
> ½ cup olive oil or salad oil
> 2 large onions, chopped
> 3 cloves garlic, minced or pressed
> 5 pounds boneless beef chuck, cut into 1½-inch cubes
> ½ cup all-purpose flour
> ¼ cup chopped fresh cilantro (coriander)
> 2 teaspoons *each* ground cumin, ground cloves, dry oregano leaves, dry rosemary, and dry tarragon
> 2 large cans (28 oz. *each*) tomatoes
> 1 can (14½ oz.) regular-strength beef broth
> Garnishes (suggestions follow)

Rinse chiles; discard stems and seeds. Break chiles into pieces. Combine chiles and water in a 2½- to 3-quart pan. Bring to a boil over high heat; reduce heat, cover, and simmer until chiles are soft (about 30 minutes).

In a blender, whirl chiles and their liquid until puréed. Rub purée through a fine wire strainer; discard residue. Set purée aside.

Heat oil in a 6- to 8-quart pan over medium heat. When oil is hot, add onions and garlic; cook, stirring often, until onions are soft (about 10 minutes). Sprinkle meat with flour. Add meat and chile purée to pan and cook, stirring, for 5 minutes.

Add cilantro, cumin, cloves, oregano, rosemary, tarragon, tomatoes (break up with a spoon) and their liquid, and broth. Bring to a boil over high heat. Reduce heat and simmer, uncovered, stirring often, until meat is very tender when pierced (3 to 4 hours).

Offer garnishes to add to individual servings. Makes about 12 servings.

Garnishes. Choose from the following, arranged in separate bowls: 2 cups (8 oz.) shredded **Cheddar cheese,** 2 cups diced **tomatoes,** and 1 large **onion,** finely chopped.

Per serving: 810 calories, 40 g protein, 21 g carbohydrates, 64 g total fat, 158 mg cholesterol, 589 mg sodium

Representing a range of savory possibilities are these two meal-in-a-bowl chilis. At left, Chili Verde (recipe on page 88) offers vibrant bell peppers, chiles, and tomatillos. Chili Colorado (recipe on facing page), at right, is meaty and spicy. Serve either one with warm tortillas and a selection of toppings.

Chili con Carne

GROUND BEEF & BEAN CHILI

Preparation time: 10 to 20 minutes
Cooking time: About 30 minutes

Actually a North American dish, chili con carne was inspired by the meat and chile stews of Mexico. This version will become a favorite.

- 1 pound lean ground beef
- 1 medium-size onion, chopped
- 2 cloves garlic, minced or pressed
- 1 large green bell pepper, chopped
- 1 tablespoon chili powder
- 1 teaspoon *each* ground cumin and dry oregano leaves
- 1 large can (15 oz.) pear-shaped tomatoes
- 1 large can (1 lb.) kidney beans, drained
- ¼ cup chopped fresh cilantro (coriander)
  - Salt
  - Garnishes (suggestions follow), optional

Crumble beef into a wide frying pan over medium-high heat; cook just until meat loses pink color (about 4 minutes); drain off fat. Add onion, garlic, and bell pepper; continue to cook, stirring, until vegetables are soft (about 10 minutes).

Stir in chili powder, cumin, oregano, and tomatoes. Bring to a boil; add beans. Reduce heat and simmer, uncovered, for 15 minutes, stirring often to break up tomatoes. Stir in cilantro and season to taste with salt. Offer garnishes, if desired, to add to individual servings. Makes 4 servings.

Garnishes. Choose from the following, arranged in separate bowls: 1 cup (4 oz.) shredded **Cheddar cheese;** 5 **green onions** (including tops), sliced; 1 firm-ripe **avocado,** diced and moistened with **lemon juice** to prevent discoloring; and ½ cup **sour cream.**

Per serving: 362 calories, 28 g protein, 26 g carbohydrates, 17 g total fat, 69 mg cholesterol, 652 mg sodium

Salpicon de Lengua

COLD TONGUE WITH VEGETABLES

Preparation time: 1 hour
Marinating time: At least 12 hours
Cooking time: 3 to 4 hours

Salpicon translates loosely into English as "salmagundi," or a potpourri of cold meats and vegetables with dressing. It's an excellent choice for an out-door lunch buffet or casual dinner. Start the dish a day ahead so the meat and vegetables can chill.

- 2½- to 3-pound beef tongue
- 2 quarts water
- 1 *each* carrot, onion, and celery stalk, sliced
- ¼ cup white wine vinegar
- 1 teaspoon salt
- ½ teaspoon black peppercorns
- 1 teaspoon dry oregano leaves
- ¼ teaspoon cumin seed
  - Tongue Marinade (recipe follows)
  - Cooked Vegetables (recipe follows)
- 1 head romaine lettuce, washed and crisped
  - Parsley sprigs
  - Sliced onion rings

Scrub tongue well under cool running water; place in a 5-quart pan. Add water, carrot, onion, celery, vinegar, salt, peppercorns, oregano, and cumin. Cover and bring to a boil; reduce heat and simmer until meat is fork-tender (2½ to 3 hours). Let cool.

Meanwhile, prepare Tongue Marinade.

Lift out tongue, reserving broth, and remove skin; trim off any fat and bones. Slice tongue thinly and place in a deep bowl. Pour marinade over meat, cover, and refrigerate for at least 12 hours or until next day.

Meanwhile, pour broth through a wire strainer into a bowl; discard residue. Skim fat from broth (or chill until fat solidifies and then lift off and discard). Prepare Cooked Vegetables, using strained broth.

Just before serving, shred lettuce and spread in a large, rimmed platter. Drain tongue and vegetables, reserving liquids. Arrange sliced tongue and vegetables on lettuce; pour over enough of the reserved liquids to moisten salad lightly. Garnish with parsley and onion rings. Makes 6 servings.

Tongue Marinade. In a medium-size bowl, combine 1 **onion,** finely chopped; ¾ cup **olive oil,** ½ cup **white wine vinegar,** ½ teaspoon **salt,** ¼ teaspoon **pepper,** and 1 teaspoon **dry oregano leaves.** Mix until blended.

Cooked Vegetables. In a 6- to 8-quart pan, bring reserved **tongue broth** to a boil. Add 6 *each* whole **carrots** and **turnips;** cover and cook until vegetables are tender (15 to 20 minutes). Remove vegetables with a slotted spoon and set aside.

Add 3 large boiling **potatoes,** cut into quarters, to broth; cover and cook until potatoes are just tender (about 20 minutes). Remove pan from heat; return carrots and turnips to pan and add ⅓ cup **olive oil** and 2 tablespoons **vinegar.** Cover and refrigerate until next day. (If stock gels, set over low heat to warm and loosen vegetables.)

Meanwhile, in a 3- to 4-quart pan, cook 3 or 4 **zucchini,** cut in half lengthwise, in boiling **salted water** to cover until tender (about 10 minutes). Drain and drop into ice water; drain again. Moisten zucchini lightly with **olive oil;** cover and refrigerate until next day.

Drain all vegetables well before arranging with meat; reserve liquid to pour over salad.

Per serving: 864 calories, 31 g protein, 46 g carbohydrates, 63 g total fat, 116 mg cholesterol, 739 mg sodium

Guisado de Picadillo
PICADILLO STEW

Preparation time: 20 minutes
Cooking time: About 35 minutes

Picadillo usually refers to a dish of ground meat seasoned with sweet and tart flavors. In this version from Jocotepec (south of Guadalajara), potatoes, tomatillos, and chunks of beef are simmered with chili sauce instead. Serve with rice for a hearty meal that's deceptively easy to prepare.

    1 pound fresh tomatillos or 1 can (13 oz.)
       tomatillos
    2 tablespoons salad oil
    1 pound boneless top round beef, thinly sliced
       across grain
    1 teaspoon cumin seeds
    1 pound thin-skinned potatoes, thinly sliced
    1 pound zucchini, ends trimmed and sliced
       ¼ inch thick
    2 cans (10 oz. *each*) red chili sauce
    1 large ripe avocado, pitted, peeled, and sliced
    3 to 4 cups hot cooked rice
       Sour cream
       Chopped fresh cilantro (coriander)

Pull off and discard husks and stems from fresh tomatillos. Rinse well and slice ¼ inch thick.

Pour oil into a 12- to 14-inch frying pan over medium-high heat. Add beef and cumin seeds and cook, stirring, until meat is no longer pink (5 minutes). Add tomatillos (if using canned tomatillos, add liquid and mash tomatillos with a spoon), potatoes, zucchini, and chili sauce. Bring to a boil; reduce heat, cover, and simmer until potatoes are soft when pierced (about 30 minutes).

For each serving, spoon hot stew over rice, garnish with avocado, and top with sour cream and cilantro. Makes 6 servings.

Per serving: 538 calories, 25 g protein, 70 g carbohydrates, 19 g total fat, 45 mg cholesterol, 1,314 mg sodium

Pierna de Cordero a la Yucateca
YUCATECAN LEG OF LAMB

Preparation time: About 25 minutes
Cooking time: 1½ to 2 hours, plus 20 minutes standing time

Have your butcher bone and butterfly a leg of lamb, then rub it with achiote, the mellow spice of the Yucatan. Use prepared achiote, available in bricks in Mexican markets; or use our chili powder and cinnamon mixture for an easy, if somewhat less colorful, substitute.

Add a citrus-cornbread stuffing and roast the festive lamb slowly on the barbecue or in the oven.

    1 tablespoon prepared achiote or ½ teaspoon
       chili powder mixed with ⅛ teaspoon ground
       cinnamon
    ½ teaspoon coarsely ground black pepper
       Salt
    2 tablespoons salad oil
       6-pound leg of lamb, boned and butterflied
    1 tablespoon grated orange peel
    3 tablespoons orange juice
    ½ teaspoon grated lemon peel
    ½ cup packed cornbread crumbs
    1 tablespoon minced onion

Blend achiote with pepper, salt, and oil. Rub over lamb.

In a bowl, mix orange peel and juice, lemon peel, cornbread crumbs, and onion. Spread mixture evenly over inside of lamb; reshape leg and skewer or tie with heavy string. Insert a meat thermometer in thickest part of meat.

To barbecue, mound and ignite 50 charcoal briquets. When coals are covered with gray ash, bank half the briquets on each side of grate. Place a metal drip pan in center of coals. Place lamb on a greased grill, 4 to 6 inches above heat, directly over drip pan. Cover barbecue and adjust dampers to maintain an even heat; cook until thermometer registers 140°F for slightly pink meat (about 2 hours) or until done to your liking.

To roast, place lamb on a rack in a large roasting pan; tent loosely with foil. Roast in a 350° oven until thermometer registers 140°F for slightly pink meat (1½ to 2 hours) or until done to your liking.

Let stand, covered with foil, for 20 minutes; slice thinly. Makes 6 to 8 servings.

Per serving: 617 calories, 52 g protein, 4 g carbohydrates, 42 g total fat, 204 mg cholesterol, 213 mg sodium

Juicy Costillar Asado (recipe on facing page) is basted with a roasted vegetable salsa made with tomatoes and mild green chiles, both also cooked on the grill. To round out a barbecue dinner, cook a few extra vegetables, including corn on the cob, to accompany the ribs. Or offer one of the stuffed chiles on page 95.

Costillar Asado

GRILLED SPARERIBS

Pictured on facing page

Preparation time: About 20 minutes
Grilling time: About 1½ hours

You do most of the cooking for this dish outside at the barbecue. Long, slow grilling is the trick to tenderizing the pork spareribs. Vegetables for the salsa basting sauce are also charred atop the grill.

- 6 **large tomatoes**
- 8 **Anaheim, Poblano, or other large mild green chiles**
- ¼ **cup** *each* **red wine vinegar and chopped fresh cilantro (coriander)**
- 3 **cloves garlic, minced or pressed**
  Salt
- 6 **to 8 pounds pork spareribs**
  Lime slices (optional)
  About 1 cup sour cream
- 3 **or 4 limes, cut into wedges**

To prepare fire, mound and ignite 50 charcoal briquets. When coals are heavily spotted with gray ash, spread to make an even layer.

Place tomatoes and chiles on a lightly greased grill 4 to 6 inches above prepared coals. Cook, turning as needed, until chiles are charred on all sides (7 to 10 minutes) and tomatoes are hot and streaked with brown (about 15 minutes).

Bank half the briquets on each side of grate, adding 5 fresh coals to each side. Place a metal drip pan in center and replace grill.

Chop grilled tomatoes and chiles, discarding stems and seeds. Place tomatoes, chiles, and their juices in a bowl. Stir in vinegar, cilantro, and garlic; season to taste with salt. Spread some of the salsa evenly over both sides of ribs; reserve remaining salsa.

Place ribs, meat sides up, on grill directly above drip pan. Cover barbecue and adjust dampers to maintain an even heat. Cook, basting occasionally with some of the remaining salsa, until meat near bone is no longer pink when slashed (1 to 1¼ hours).

Cut ribs into 2- to 3-rib portions; garnish with lime slices, if desired. Offer remaining salsa, sour cream, and lime wedges to add to individual servings. Makes 6 to 8 servings.

Per serving: 632 calories, 41 g protein, 12 g carbohydrates, 47 g total fat, 173 mg cholesterol, 151 mg sodium

Guisado de Puerco con Verdolaga

PORK STEW WITH PURSLANE

Preparation time: About 25 minutes
Cooking time: About 3 hours

A sprawling, mildly tart-flavored weed, purslane sometimes appears in Mexican markets under the name *verdolaga*. Fresh spinach works just as well.

- 4½ **to 5 pounds boneless pork shoulder**
- 4 **cloves garlic**
- 2 **cups water**
  Tomatillo Sauce (recipe follows)
  Salt
  About 1½ lbs. purslane (*verdolaga*) sprigs or lightly packed spinach leaves
- 3 **quarts boiling water**

Trim excess fat from pork; reserve for Tomatillo Sauce. Cut meat into 1½-inch cubes. In a 5- to 6-quart ovenproof pan, combine meat with garlic and water. Bring to a boil over high heat; reduce heat, cover, and simmer for 45 minutes.

Remove from heat and ladle out 2 cups of the broth; reserve for sauce. Place pan, uncovered, in a 425° oven. Bake, stirring often, until well browned (about 1 hour). Meanwhile, prepare Tomatillo Sauce; set aside.

Place pan over medium heat; add sauce and season to taste with salt. Stir to free browned bits. Bring to a boil over high heat; reduce heat, cover, and simmer until meat is very tender when pierced (about 1 hour). At this point, you may cool, cover, and refrigerate for up to 3 days. Reheat to a simmer before continuing.

Rinse purslane well; drain. Pour boiling water over greens and let stand until wilted. Drain again.

Ladle stew into bowls; top with greens. Makes 8 to 10 servings.

Tomatillo Sauce. In a blender or food processor, combine 3 cans (13 oz. *each*) **tomatillos,** drained, and 4 **fresh or canned jalapeño chiles,** stemmed and seeded. Whirl until puréed; set aside.

In a 12- to 14-inch frying pan over medium heat, render ¼ cup fat from **reserved pork fat;** discard extra fat. Add 4 large **onions,** sliced, and 3 cloves **garlic,** minced or pressed. Cook, stirring, until onions are golden. Add 2 cups **reserved broth;** boil, uncovered, until almost all broth has evaporated. Pour in tomatillo mixture.

Per serving: 382 calories, 38 g protein, 12 g carbohydrates, 20 g total fat, 125 mg cholesterol, 169 mg sodium

Cochinita Pibil

YUCATECAN PORK IN BANANA LEAVES *compare*

Preparation time: About 30 minutes, plus about 12 hours to soak achiote seeds
Marinating time: At least 8 hours
Baking time: 3 to 3½ hours

Cooking foods in banana leaves (a style called *pibil*) and flavoring meats with achiote are culinary arts unique to Mexico's Yucatan peninsula. Look for refrigerated banana leaves and packaged achiote (annatto) seeds in Mexican markets. Ti leaves can be obtained from most florists; use foil if neither kind of leaf is available.

- ⅔ **cup Achiote Paste (recipe follows)**
  3½- to 4-pound boneless pork shoulder
  Banana Leaves (directions follow), ti leaves, stemmed, or foil, cut or arranged to make a 12- by 20-inch rectangle
- 8 **to 10 flour tortillas (7- to 9-inch diameter)**
  Salsa Fresca, homemade (page 48) or purchased

Prepare Achiote Paste; set aside. Make ½-inch-deep cuts in fat side of pork. Prepare Banana Leaves and place meat in center. Spread paste over roast, rubbing into cuts. Fold leaves to enclose meat; tie securely. Refrigerate for at least 8 hours or until next day.

Place a rack in bottom of a deep 6- to 8-quart pan; pour in 1½ cups water and place roast on rack. Cover and bake in a 350° oven until roast is very tender when pierced through leaves (3 to 3½ hours); add hot water as needed. Stack tortillas, wrap in foil, and heat with pork during last 15 minutes. Prepare Salsa Fresca.

Place roast on a board. Slit packet open lengthwise; peel back leaves. Pour pan juices over meat (if you used foil, discard juices). Pull off pieces of pork to pile on flour tortillas and top with salsa. Makes 8 to 10 servings.

Achiote Paste. Place 2 ounces (⅓ cup) **achiote (annatto) seeds** in a bowl with enough **boiling water** to cover; cover tightly and let stand until soft (about 12 hours).

Drain; discard liquid. In a blender, combine seeds with 1 tablespoon **ground cumin;** 1 teaspoon **coarsely ground black pepper;** 2 teaspoons **ground allspice;** 2 tablespoons chopped **garlic;** 2 **small dried hot red chiles,** torn into pieces; ½ teaspoon **salt;** and 6 tablespoons *each* **orange juice** and **white wine vinegar.** Whirl until smooth (2 to 3 minutes). If made ahead, cover and refrigerate for up to 10 days; freeze for longer storage. Makes about 1 cup.

Banana Leaves. Thoroughly rinse enough refrigerated or frozen thawed **banana leaves** to make a 12- by 20-inch rectangle. Pat dry. Glide flat surface of leaves across gas flame or electric element (on high) of your range for a few seconds until leaves become shiny and more flexible.

Per serving: 573 calories, 30 g protein, 28 g carbohydratges, 37 g total fat, 114 mg cholesterol, 532 mg sodium

Chuletas de Puerco

CHILI PORK STEAKS

Preparation time: About 20 minutes
Marinating time: At least 2 hours
Cooking time: About 10 minutes

Although it's a thrifty alternative to many cuts of beef, pork steaks often dry out during cooking. Rubbing them with a marinade enhances their flavor, while quick pan-frying seals in moisture.

- 4 **pork shoulder steaks (about 6 oz. *each*), cut ½ inch thick**
- 1½ **tablespoons chili powder**
- 1 **teaspoon *each* dry oregano leaves and garlic salt**
- ¼ **teaspoon ground cumin**
- 3 **tablespoons wine vinegar**
- 3 **tablespoons salad oil**
  Green Chile Salsa (recipe follows)

Trim and discard excess fat from steaks; set aside. In a small bowl, combine chili powder, oregano, garlic salt, cumin, vinegar, and 1 tablespoon of the oil. Rub mixture on both sides of steaks. Cover and refrigerate for at least 2 hours or until next day. Meanwhile, prepare Green Chile Salsa; cover and refrigerate.

Heat remaining 2 tablespoons oil in a wide frying pan over medium-high heat. When oil is hot, add steaks and cook, turning once, until no longer pink when cut in thickest part (about 10 minutes total).

Serve with salsa. Makes 4 servings.

Green Chile Salsa. Combine 1 large **tomato,** chopped; 1 small **onion,** chopped; 1 small can (4 oz.) **diced green chiles;** and 1 tablespoon **vinegar.** Mix until blended.

Per serving: 313 calories, 25 g protein, 7 g carbohydrates, 21 g total fat, 83 mg cholesterol, 762 mg sodium

Poc Chuc

BARBECUED PORK IN ORANGE SAUCE

Preparation time: About 20 minutes
Marinating time: 1 hour
Cooking time: 40 to 50 minutes

Sour orange, native to the Yucatan, is often used as a tart marinade for pork. Because this tropical citrus is unavailable here, we approximate the flavor with Valencia oranges and lemon juice. Served with hot rice and tomato sauce, it becomes a complete regional menu.

thick
(use Valencia oranges)

ipe follows), optional

ed

ional)

chops. In a large
emon juice, and salt.
hour, turning several

Tomato Sauce, if

reserving marinade,
ches above a bed
os, turning once,
hen cut (20 to 30

wide frying pan
and cook, stirring,
minutes). Add
a boil. Remove

d garnish with
onions from sauce
tro; offer remain-
l to add to indi-
rice topped with
servings.

spoons **salad oil**
high heat. Add
stirring, until
bell peppers,

seeded and diced, and 2 large **tomatoes,** seeded and diced. Simmer gently until thickened (about 10 minutes). Remove from heat. Serve warm or at room temperature.

Per serving: 440 calories, 29 g protein, 20 g carbohydrates, 29 g total fat, 95 mg cholesterol, 258 mg sodium

Guisado de Puerco con Tomatillos

PORK STEW WITH TOMATILLOS

Preparation time: About 20 minutes
Cooking time: About 1¼ hours

Tomatillos add piquancy to this lively stew. Serve it as you would a chili, garnished with sour cream and cilantro and accompanied by warm tortillas and beer.

- 2½ **pounds boneless pork shoulder**
- 2 **tablespoons salad oil**
- 1 **large onion, chopped**
- 2 **cloves garlic, minced or pressed**
- 1½ **cups chopped fresh or canned and drained tomatillos**
- 1 **large can (7 oz.) diced green chiles**
- 1 **teaspoon dry marjoram leaves**
- ¼ **cup chopped fresh cilantro (coriander)**
- ½ **cup water**
  Salt
  Sour cream
  Cilantro (coriander) sprigs

Trim and discard fat from pork; cut pork into 1-inch cubes.

Heat oil in a wide 3- to 4-quart pan over medium-high heat. Add meat, a few pieces at a time, and cook until lightly browned on all sides. Lift out meat, transfer to a plate, and keep warm; reserve drippings in pan.

Add onion to pan and cook, stirring, until soft (about 7 minutes). Return meat to pan and stir in garlic, tomatillos, chiles, marjoram, chopped cilantro, and water. Season to taste with salt. Cover and simmer until meat is tender when pierced (about 1 hour). Skim off fat.

Spoon into serving bowls and garnish with sour cream and cilantro sprigs. Makes 4 to 6 servings.

Per serving: 362 calories, 38 g protein, 6 g carbohydrates, 20 g total fat, 127 mg cholesterol, 347 mg sodium

Salchichas en Hojas de Maiz
CORN-HUSK SAUSAGES

Pictured on facing page

Preparation time: About 1 hour, plus at least 20 minutes to soak corn husks
Cooking time: 15 to 30 minutes

Wrapped in corn husks, fresh sausages were never easier. Nor have they ever tasted so good—succulent, tender, and spicy, with just the right touch of Mexican seasonings.

	About 3 ounces dried corn husks
	Smoky Roasted Salsa (page 49) or purchased red salsa
2	pounds lean ground pork
1	medium-size onion, minced
1	cup fine dry bread crumbs
2	large eggs
¼	cup ground chile powder
⅓	cup red wine vinegar
3	cloves garlic, minced or pressed
2	teaspoons cumin seeds
1	teaspoon dry oregano leaves
	About 1½ teaspoons salt
	Cilantro (coriander) sprigs

Separate and sort corn husks, discarding silk and other extraneous material. Place husks in a large dish and cover with warm water; let stand until pliable (at least 20 minutes) or until next day.

Prepare Smoky Roasted Salsa; set aside. Mix pork, onion, bread crumbs, eggs, chiles, vinegar, garlic, cumin seeds, oregano, and 1½ teaspoons of the salt. Poach a spoonful of the mixture to taste for salt and add more salt, if necessary.

Drain husks and shake off excess water. Tear a few husks along grain to make ¼-inch-wide strips for tying sausage. For each sausage, select a wide, pliable corn husk. Lay flat and spoon ¼ cup of the pork filling down a long side of husk; form into a 4-inch-long log with about 2 inches of husk exposed on each end. Starting on filled side, roll husk up and tie ends with strips; if husk is not wide enough to wrap around filling, overlap with another husk. (At this point, you may cover filled husks and refrigerate for up to a day).

Place a rack or steaming basket in a 5- to 6-quart pan; pour in water to a depth of 1 inch (water should not touch rack). Bring to a boil; arrange half the sausages on rack. Cover and cook over high heat until filling is firm to touch and pork is no longer pink when cut in center (about 15 minutes).

Repeat for remaining sausages, adding boiling water to pan as needed to maintain water level (or cook all sausages at once in stacking steamer baskets).

Untie husk strips and open wrappers; garnish with cilantro sprigs and offer salsa to spoon on individual servings. Makes 6 to 8 servings (about 24 sausages).

Per sausage: 273 calories, 25 g protein, 13 g carbohydrates, 13 g total fat, 146 mg cholesterol, 603 mg sodium

Pollo a la Naranja
CHICKEN WITH ORANGES

Preparation time: About 15 minutes
Cooking time: About 1 hour

Spices, raisins, and citrus embellish chicken with tropical flavors. Serve with mellow Black Beans (page 89) and a simple green salad.

	3½-pound frying chicken, cut up
⅛	teaspoon *each* ground cinnamon and ground cloves
	Salt and pepper
3	tablespoons salad oil
2	cloves garlic, minced or pressed
1	medium-size onion, chopped
1	cup orange juice
	Pinch of ground saffron
2	tablespoons seedless raisins
1	tablespoon capers
½	cup coarsely chopped almonds
3	oranges, peel and white membrane discarded, sliced

Rinse chicken and pat dry. Sprinkle with cinnamon and cloves; season to taste with salt and pepper. Heat oil in a wide frying pan over medium-high heat. When oil is hot, add chicken, several pieces at a time, and cook until well browned on all sides (about 10 minutes). Repeat for remaining chicken, setting aside as cooked. Discard all but 2 tablespoons of the drippings and add garlic and onion; cook, stirring, until vegetables are soft (about 7 minutes).

Return chicken to pan with orange juice, saffron, raisins, and capers. Cover and cook over low heat until meat near thighbone is no longer pink when slashed (about 35 minutes). Stir in almonds. Garnish individual servings with orange slices. Makes 4 to 6 servings.

Per serving: 510 calories, 35 g protein, 19 g carbohydrates, 33 g total fat, 106 mg cholesterol, 135 mg sodium

Sausage-making is a snap if, instead of using casings, you roll a delicious pork filling into dampened corn husks (the same as those used for tamales). Then, you can steam several Salchichas en Hojas de Maiz (recipe on facing page) at once. Offer Smoky Roasted Salsa (recipe on page 49) to spoon over the mild-flavored sausages.

Pollo en Mole Poblano

CHICKEN IN MOLE SAUCE

Preparation time: About 45 minutes
Cooking time: About 1 hour

Legend tells that, centuries ago in the town of Puebla, sisters at a local convent expected a visit by an important dignitary. Desperate for a dish worthy of their guest, they invented this complex sauce for fowl. Acclaimed for its wonderful flavor then, *mole poblano* remains the pride of Puebla today. Try it with turkey for a special holiday treat.

''Mole'' refers to a whole category of sauces; mole poblano always includes its signature ingredient: chocolate. A green mole, made with tomatillos, is also delicious with chicken.

> 2 **frying chickens (about 3 lbs. *each*), cut up**
> 1 **large onion, sliced**
> 3 **whole cloves garlic**
>   **About 3 cups regular-strength chicken broth**
>   **Mole Sauce (recipe follows)**
> 4 **to 6 cups hot cooked rice**
> ¼ **cup minced fresh cilantro (coriander)**

In a large pan, combine chicken legs, thighs, and wings with onion, garlic, and 2 cups of the broth. Cover and simmer for 25 minutes. Split breasts and add to pan; continue to simmer, covered, until meat near thighbone is no longer pink when slashed (about 20 more minutes).

Remove chicken from broth; let cool slightly. Leave pieces whole, or discard skin and bones and cut meat into large chunks.

Strain broth and discard vegetables; skim and discard fat from broth. Add enough additional broth to make 4 cups total. (At this point, you may cover and refrigerate chicken and broth separately for up to a day.)

Prepare Mole Sauce and pour into a 4- to 5-quart pan; bring to a boil over high heat. Reduce heat, add chicken, and simmer until meat is hot. Place hot rice on a serving platter; with a slotted spoon, transfer chicken to platter. Drizzle with enough sauce to lightly coat; sprinkle with cilantro. Offer remaining sauce in a separate bowl to add to individual servings. Makes 6 to 8 servings.

Mole Sauce. Arrange 1 **ancho chile**, 1 **pasilla chile**, and 1 **dried New Mexico chile** on a large baking sheet. Bake in a 350° oven until chiles smell toasted (about 10 minutes). Discard stems and seeds; grind chiles to a powder in a blender (or substitute ¼ cup ground chile powder for roasted, ground chiles).

To blender add 20 **blanched almonds**; ¼ cup diced **green-tipped banana**; 1 teaspoon **ground cinnamon**; 1 clove **garlic**; 2 **corn tortillas**, torn into pieces; 2 tablespoons **sesame seeds**; 1 tablespoon **pine nuts**; and 1 cup of the **reserved chicken broth**; whirl until puréed. (Sauce will be grainy.)

Pour into a pan; add 6 tablespoons **butter** or margarine, 1 ounce **semisweet chocolate,** and remaining **chicken broth.** Heat to a simmer, stirring; then season to taste with **salt**, if desired.

Per serving: 727 calories, 48 g protein, 38 g carbohydrates, 43 g total fat, 176 mg cholesterol, 735 mg sodium

TURKEY IN MOLE SAUCE

Pictured on page 30

Prepare **Mole Sauce** as directed for **Chicken in Mole Sauce** (at left), using 4 cups **regular-strength chicken broth.** In a 4- to 5-quart pan, combine sauce with 6 cups **cooked, boned turkey,** cut into 3-inch pieces. Simmer over medium heat until meat is hot. Serve on a platter with **Arroz Blanco** (page 92). Garnish with ¼ cup minced **fresh cilantro** (coriander). Makes 6 to 8 servings.

Per serving: 359 calories, 34 g protein, 12 g carbohydrates, 20 g total fat, 104 mg cholesterol, 670 mg sodium

CHICKEN IN GREEN MOLE

Cook 1 **frying chicken** (about 3 lbs.) as directed for **Chicken in Mole Sauce** (at left), reserving broth. Whirl 2 cans (13 oz. *each*) **tomatillos** and their liquid in a blender until smooth; set aside. Heat 2 tablespoons **salad oil** in a wide frying pan over medium-high heat. Add 1 **onion,** finely chopped, and ¼ cup finely chopped **almonds** and cook, stirring, until almonds are lightly browned. Add tomatillo purée, 1 tablespoon minced **fresh cilantro** (coriander), 3 tablespoons **canned diced green chiles,** and **reserved chicken broth.** Boil rapidly until reduced to 2½ cups.

Skin and bone chicken and cut into large chunks. Arrange in a wide frying pan. Pour in sauce, cover, and simmer until meat is hot (about 10 minutes). Transfer to a rimmed platter lined with **small lettuce leaves** and garnish with **sour cream.** Makes 4 to 6 servings.

Per serving: 405 calories, 32 g protein, 9 g carbohydrates, 27 g total fat, 102 mg cholesterol, 641 mg sodium

Pollo en Escabeche

CHICKEN IN ESCABECHE SAUCE

Preparation time: About 25 minutes
Cooking time: About 1 hour

Potent with spices and garlic, escabeche sauce seasons tender baked chicken before it's quickly grilled to crisp the skin. Use leftover paste for Chilled Fish in Escabeche (page 80).

- 2½ tablespoons Escabeche Paste (recipe follows)
  - 3½- to 4-pound frying chicken, cut up
- 1½ cups regular-strength chicken broth
- 1 tablespoon salad oil
- 2 large onions, thinly sliced
- 1 large can (7 oz.) diced green chiles
- 1½ tablespoons cornstarch mixed with 1½ tablespoons water
- 3 tablespoons chopped fresh cilantro (coriander)

Prepare Escabeche Paste. Rinse chicken and pat dry. Using a sharp knife, deeply pierce chicken all over. Rub paste on chicken, pushing some under skin. Place in a 9- by 13-inch baking pan; pour in broth. Cover and bake in a 400° oven until chicken is tender when pierced (about 40 minutes).

Lift chicken from broth; drain briefly. Skim and discard fat from broth; reserve broth. Place chicken on a lightly greased grill 4 to 6 inches above a solid bed of medium-hot coals. Cook, turning as needed, until well browned (10 to 15 minutes). Or place drained chicken on a preheated broiler pan 4 to 6 inches below heat. Broil, turning once, until well browned (6 to 8 minutes).

Meanwhile, heat oil in a wide frying pan over medium heat. When oil is hot, add onions and cook, stirring, until soft (about 10 minutes). Stir in chiles, reserved broth, and cornstarch mixture. Continue to cook, stirring, until sauce boils and thickens. Stir in cilantro. Spoon sauce over individual servings of chicken. Makes 4 to 6 servings.

Escabeche Paste. Combine 8 cloves **garlic,** minced or pressed; 1 teaspoon *each* **ground allspice, ground cloves, ground cumin,** and **ground coriander;** 1½ teaspoons **ground cinnamon;** ¾ teaspoon **coarsely ground black pepper;** 2 teaspoons **dry oregano leaves;** ¼ teaspoon **ground red pepper** (cayenne); and 2 tablespoons *each* **orange juice** and **white wine vinegar.** Mix until blended. If made ahead, cover and refrigerate for up to 2 weeks. Makes ¼ cup.

Per serving: 351 calories, 34 g protein, 11 g carbohydrates, 19 g total fat, 103 mg cholesterol, 552 mg sodium

Pollo Nogalense

NOGALES BAKED CHICKEN

Preparation time: About 15 minutes
Baking time: 30 to 45 minutes

In the border town of Nogales, the culinary traditions of Mexico and Arizona are blended. This baked chicken is a tongue-tingling sample of the result.

- Tomatillo Salsa (page 49) or purchased green chile salsa
- 3 whole chicken breasts (about 1 lb. *each*), skinned, boned, and split, or 12 chicken thighs (3 to 3½ lbs. *total*), skinned
- 2 eggs
- 1 clove garlic, minced or pressed
- 1½ cups fine dry bread crumbs
- 2 teaspoons *each* chili powder and ground cumin
- ½ teaspoon ground oregano
- 6 tablespoons butter or margarine
- 1 large ripe avocado
- 4 to 6 cups shredded romaine lettuce leaves
  - About 1 cup plain yogurt or sour cream
  - About 6 tablespoons thinly sliced green onions (including tops)
- 12 to 18 cherry tomatoes
- 1 or 2 limes, cut into wedges

Prepare Tomatillo Salsa; set aside. Rinse chicken and pat dry. Set aside.

In a shallow bowl, beat together eggs, garlic, and ¼ cup of the salsa. In another shallow bowl, combine bread crumbs, chili powder, cumin, and oregano. Dip each chicken piece in egg mixture; drain briefly. Then coat with crumb mixture and shake off excess.

In a rimmed 10- to 15-inch baking pan, melt butter in a 375° oven. Add chicken; turn to coat with butter. Bake, uncovered, until meat in thickest part is no longer pink when slashed (30 to 35 minutes for breasts, about 45 minutes for thighs).

Pit, peel, and slice avocado. Arrange chicken on a bed of shredded lettuce on a serving platter and top each piece with a dollop of yogurt. Garnish with avocado, green onions, tomatoes, and lime wedges; offer remaining yogurt and salsa in separate bowls to add to individual servings. Makes 6 servings.

Per serving: 503 calories, 43 g protein, 29 g carbohydrates, 24 g total fat, 211 mg cholesterol, 476 mg sodium

*A banana leaf enfolding tender chicken seasoned with mellow achiote
captures the flavors of the Yucatan in Mexico's classic Pollo Pibil
(recipe on facing page). When you shop for the achiote at a Mexican market,
also bring home some tropical fruits and plantains to serve alongside.*

Pato en Pipian

DUCKLING IN PIPIAN SAUCE

Preparation time: About 40 minutes

sed in many dishes,
pumpkin seeds
ere it accents crisp
h roast chicken or
with Arroz Blanco
8).

follows)
each), thawed if

peño chiles or other
ed, seeded, and

pped
pressed
ntro (coriander)
resh epazote or 2
crumbled (optional)
drained
leaves, torn into pieces

chicken broth

aside.

dry. Discard excess fat;
ses. Place ducks, breast
large roasting pan. Bake,
for 1 hour. Turn ducks
til skin is crisp and meat
leg bone (about 1 more

nder, combine chiles,
pazote, tomatillos, and
ooth.

quart pan over medium
dd chile purée and pipian
ntil sauce bubbles. Blend
boil.

rs, cut ducks in half or in
nto a rimmed serving platter;
kes 4 to 8 servings.

12 ounces (2½ cups) **hulled,**
eeds on a large rimmed baking
once or twice, in a 350° oven
rown (12 to 15 minutes).

In a blender, combine seeds with 2 cups
regular-strength chicken broth; 2 fresh or canned
jalapeño chiles, stemmed and seeded; 1 teaspoon
each **ground cumin, ground white pepper,** and **salt;**
1 tablespoon chopped **fresh epazote** or 1 teaspoon
dry epazote, if desired; and ¼ cup chopped **fresh
cilantro** (coriander). Whirl until smooth. (Sauce
will be grainy.) If made ahead, cover and refrigerate
for up to 5 days; freeze for longer storage. Makes
about 3 ½ cups.

*Per serving: 772 calories, 41 g protein, 5 g carbohydrates,
65 g total fat, 163 mg cholesterol, 394 mg sodium*

Pollo Pibil ~~compare~~

CHICKEN IN BANANA LEAVES

Pictured on facing page

*Preparation time: 30 minutes, plus about 12 hours to soak
achiote seeds*
Marinating time: At least 8 hours
Baking time: About 2 hours

Like Cochinita Pibil (page 72), this Yucatecan
specialty presents the ancient and exotic flavors
of banana leaf and achiote. (One batch of achiote
paste is enough for both recipes.)

- 5½ tablespoons Achiote Paste (page 72)
- 2 tablespoons salad oil
- 1 large onion, cut into ½-inch-thick slices
- 2 large tomatoes, cut into ½-inch-thick slices
  3½- to 4-pound frying chicken, cut into quarters
- 4 Banana Leaves (page 72) or 4 sheets foil, *each* 12 by 15 inches; or 8 ti leaves, stemmed
- ¼ cup boiling water

Prepare Achiote Paste; set aside. Heat oil in a wide
frying pan over medium heat. When oil is hot,
add onion and cook, stirring, until soft (about 5
minutes). Add tomatoes and 1½ tablespoons of
the paste; continue to cook, stirring gently, until
tomatoes are soft (1 to 2 minutes).

Rinse chicken and pat dry. Using a sharp knife,
deeply pierce chicken all over. Rub 1 tablespoon of
the paste on each quarter; place each on a banana
leaf (or 2 overlapping ti leaves) and top with a
quarter of the tomato mixture.

Fold leaves around chicken; tie securely.
Refrigerate for at least 8 hours or until next day.

Arrange bundles in a 9- by 13-inch baking dish;
pour in water. Cover and bake in a 300° oven until
chicken is tender when pierced through leaves (1½
to 1 ¾ hours). Slit leaf packets and peel back leaves.
Increase oven temperature to 450° and continue
baking, uncovered, until chicken is browned
(about 10 more minutes). Makes 4 servings.

*Per serving: 697 calories, 53 g protein, 12 g carbohydrates,
49 g total fat, 203 mg cholesterol, 483 mg sodium*

Camarones al Mojo de Ajo

SHRIMP WITH GARLIC BUTTER

Preparation time: About 10 minutes
Grilling time: About 6 minutes

Plump shrimp abound along Mexico's coastline. One of the most succulent treatments is to grill them until pink and juicy while basting with a fragrant garlic-butter sauce. Enjoy as an appetizer or a main dish.

 2 pounds medium-size shrimp, peeled and deveined
 ½ cup (¼ lb.) butter or margarine
 ½ cup olive oil
 3 cloves garlic, minced or pressed
 3 tablespoons minced parsley
 2 tablespoons lemon juice

Rinse shrimp and thread on skewers through tail section and thicker end, arranging 4 to 6 shrimp on each skewer. If using wooden skewers, be sure to soak in water for at least 12 hours to prevent burning.

In a small pan, melt butter over medium heat. Add oil, garlic, and parsley. Cook until just bubbling; remove from heat. Baste skewered shrimp with butter mixture and place on a grill 4 to 6 inches above a solid bed of medium-hot coals; or place shrimp on a rack in a broiler pan 4 inches below heat. Grill until shrimp turn bright pink (about 3 minutes), basting at least once with butter mixture. Turn shrimp, baste again, and continue to grill until opaque in center when cut (2 to 3 more minutes).

Arrange shrimp on a serving platter. Heat remaining baste with lemon juice; pour into small containers. Offer for dipping. Makes 4 to 8 servings.

Per serving: 321 calories, 19 g protein, 2 g carbohydrates, 27 g total fat, 171 mg cholesterol, 255 mg sodium

Pescado en Escabeche

CHILLED FISH IN ESCABECHE

Preparation time: About 30 minutes
Cooking time: About 50 minutes
Chilling time: At least 8 hours

Escabeche takes the role of a pickling sauce in this intriguing cold fish dish. An extraordinary first course or light main dish, it needs only tortilla chips (page 41) and fresh fruit for dessert.

 4 teaspoons Escabeche Paste (page 77)
 ⅓ cup olive oil or salad oil
 2 cloves garlic, minced or pressed
 ⅓ cup *each* orange juice and white wine vinegar
 ⅔ cup regular-strength chicken broth
 2 teaspoons sugar
 2 bay leaves
  About 2 pounds fish fillets or steaks (such as red snapper, halibut, or swordfish)
 1 large red onion, sliced and separated into rings
 1 small can (4 oz.) whole green chiles, drained and seeded
  Spinach leaves
 ½ cup fresh cilantro (coriander) leaves

Prepare Escabeche Paste. Heat 1 tablespoon of the oil in a 2- to 3-quart pan over medium heat. When oil is hot, add paste and garlic. Cook, stirring, for 1 minute. Gradually stir in orange juice, vinegar, broth, sugar, and bay leaves; bring to a boil over high heat. Reduce heat and keep warm.

Fold fillets in half to form 1-inch-thick pieces. Heat 3 more tablespoons of the oil in a wide frying pan over medium heat. When oil is hot, add fish in a single layer. Cook, turning once, until fish is golden brown and just slightly translucent or wet inside when cut (8 to 10 minutes total). Repeat for remaining fish, adding more oil as needed.

Arrange fish in a 9-inch square baking dish; top with onion. Spoon escabeche mixture over fish. Cover and refrigerate for at least 8 hours or until next day, spooning marinade over fish several times.

Lay chiles on a rimmed platter; surround with spinach. Arrange fish on chiles; top with onion and cilantro. Spoon marinade over all. Makes 6 to 8 servings.

Per serving: 221 calories, 24 g protein, 6 g carbohydrates, 11 g total fat, 42 mg cholesterol, 245 mg sodium

Cazuela de Pescados

HOT OR COLD FISH STEW

Preparation time: About 15 minutes
Cooking time: 25 to 30 minutes

Light and zesty, this fish stew delights the palate whether served hot or cold. Colorful nasturtium blossoms, available at specialty produce stores, make a nippy garnish. Serve with the same white wine you use in the stew.

1¼ **pounds tomatillos, husked**
1 **fresh jalapeño or other small hot chile, stemmed**
1 **small onion, chopped**
1 **cup fresh corn kernels**
2 **tablespoons salad oil**
3 **cups regular-strength chicken broth**
½ **cup slightly sweet white wine (such as Gewürztraminer)**
1 **pound boneless, firm-textured fish (such as sea bass, monkfish, or halibut), cut into bite-size pieces**
½ **cup chopped parsley**
Nasturtium blossoms, well washed (optional)

Rinse tomatillos. Thinly slice 3 medium-size (1½-inch diameter) tomatillos; chop remaining tomatillos. Thinly slice chile.

In a 5- to 6-quart pan, combine chopped tomatillos, chile slices, onion, corn, and oil. Cook, uncovered, stirring occasionally, over medium-high heat until mixture begins to brown (20 to 25 minutes).

Add broth and wine. Cover and bring to a boil over high heat. Add fish and sliced tomatillos. Remove from heat and let stand until fish is just slightly translucent or wet inside when cut in thickest part (1 to 2 minutes). Serve warm; or let cool, cover, and refrigerate until chilled or for up to a day.

Stir in parsley just before serving. Ladle into bowls; top with nasturtiums, if desired. Makes 4 servings.

Per serving: 270 calories, 26 g protein, 16 g carbohydrates, 12 g total fat, 47 mg cholesterol, 841 mg sodium

Ostiones Pimentados
PEPPERED OYSTERS

Preparation time: 10 minutes
Cooking time: About 5 minutes

Oysters cooked in a pungent lime and pepper sauce are perfect with Margaritas (page 124).

2 **dozen shucked oysters, drained and rinsed**
2 **tablespoons salad oil**
2 **cloves garlic, minced or pressed**
2 **teaspoons freshly ground black pepper**
3 **tablespoons lime juice**
Fried Tortilla Chips, homemade (page 41) or purchased

Pat oysters dry and set aside. Heat oil in an 8- to 10-inch frying pan over medium-high heat. Add

garlic and pepper and cook, stirring, until fragrant (about 1 minute). Add oysters and cook, stirring constantly, until edges curl (about 3 minutes). Pour in lime juice and boil until sauce thickens. Pour oysters into small bowls. Serve with tortilla chips. Makes 2 to 4 servings.

Per serving: 126 calories, 6 g protein, 5 g carbohydrates, 9 g total fat, 47 mg cholesterol, 98 mg sodium

Zarzuela
FISH & RICE STEW

Preparation time: About 20 minutes
Cooking time: About 35 minutes

Popular along Mexico's coastline, this stew has as many versions as there are fishing villages.

6 **tablespoons salad oil**
3 **large onions, finely chopped**
1 **cup lightly packed minced parsley**
2 **cups rice**
1 **large can (28 oz.) pear-shaped tomatoes**
2 **bottles (8 oz. *each*) clam juice**
2 **cups water**
¼ **cup chopped fresh cilantro (coriander)**
2½ **pounds boneless, skinless white-fleshed fish fillets (such as halibut, rockfish, or sea bass), cut into 1½-inch pieces**
½ **pound scallops, cut into ½-inch pieces if large**
¾ **pound tiny whole cooked shrimp**
Garnishes (directions follow)

Heat oil in a 5- to 6-quart pan over medium-high heat. When oil is hot, add onions; cook, stirring, until onions are soft (about 7 minutes). Stir in parsley and rice and cook until rice is slightly toasted (about 3 more minutes). Add tomatoes (break up with a spoon) and their liquid, clam juice, water, and cilantro. Bring to a boil; reduce heat, cover, and simmer for 15 minutes.

Stir in fish chunks, scallops, and shrimp; cook, covered, over low heat until fish is just slightly translucent or wet inside when cut and rice is tender to bite (about 10 minutes). Spoon into a wide shallow serving dish. Garnish as directed. Makes 6 to 8 servings.

Garnishes. Pit, peel, and slice 1 large **avocado** and arrange in center of zarzuela; quarter 4 **limes** and arrange around edge of dish. Slice 2 **green onions** (including tops) and sprinkle over all.

Per serving: 587 calories, 49 g protein, 53 g carbohydrates, 20 g total fat, 138 mg cholesterol, 518 mg sodium

Huachinango a la Veracruzana

SNAPPER VERACRUZ

Preparation time: About 15 minutes
Cooking time: 30 to 35 minutes

Perhaps the most celebrated of Mexican fish dishes, this snapper recipe comes from the pretty seacoast town for which it's named. The many versions offered throughout Mexico always include capers, olives, and tomatoes. Use red snapper or rockfish.

- ¼ **cup olive oil**
- 1 **small green bell pepper, chopped**
- 1 **medium-size onion, chopped**
- 3 **cloves garlic, minced or pressed**
- ¼ **teaspoon ground white pepper**
- 1 **teaspoon ground cinnamon**
  Juice of 1 lime
- ½ **cup sliced pimento-stuffed green olives**
- ¼ **cup canned diced green chiles**
- 3 **large tomatoes, seeded and coarsely chopped**
- 4 **snapper or rockfish fillets (about 2 lbs.** *total***)**
- 1 **tablespoon capers, rinsed**

Heat oil in a large frying pan over medium-high heat. When oil is hot, add bell pepper, onion, and garlic and cook until soft (about 7 minutes). Add pepper, cinnamon, lime juice, olives, and chiles; cook for 1 more minute. Add tomatoes and bring mixture to a boil; cook until thickened (about 10 minutes).

Place fillets in a lightly greased baking dish just large enough to hold them. Pour sauce over fish and bake in a 350° oven until fish is just slightly translucent or wet inside when cut in thickest part (10 to 15 minutes). Stir in capers just before serving. Makes 4 servings.

Per serving: 407 calories, 48 g protein, 10 g carbohydrates, 19 g total fat, 84 mg cholesterol, 671 mg sodium

Salmon en Salsa Verde

SALMON WITH CILANTRO SALSA

Pictured on facing page

Preparation time: About 10 minutes
Baking time: 35 to 45 minutes

Vivid green and tart flavored, cilantro sauce perfectly accents the exquisite pink flesh of salmon.

- 2 **large unskinned salmon fillets (about 4 lbs.** *total***)**
- ¾ **cup lime juice**
- ⅔ **cup thinly sliced green onions (including tops)**
- 2 **pickled jalapeño chiles, stemmed and finely chopped**
- 1½ **cups loosely packed fresh cilantro (coriander) leaves, minced**
- ⅓ **cup olive oil**

Lay fillets, skin sides down, in a 9- by 13-inch baking dish. Evenly drizzle 2 tablespoons of the lime juice over fillets.

In a small bowl, combine remaining lime juice, green onions, chiles, cilantro, and olive oil. Spread ½ cup of the cilantro mixture over a fillet; lay other fillet, skin side up, atop first. (At this point, you may cover and refrigerate for up to a day.)

Bake, uncovered, in a 350° oven until fish is just slightly translucent or wet inside when cut in thickest part (35 to 45 minutes). If desired, pull off top skin; slice through fish just down to bottom fillet and lift off portions with a spatula. Spoon remaining salsa over individual servings. Makes 8 to 10 servings.

Per serving: 328 calories, 36 g protein, 2 g carbohydrates, 19 g total fat, 100 mg cholesterol, 128 mg sodium

Pez Espada a la Baja

SWORDFISH BAJA-STYLE

Preparation time: 10 minutes
Baking time: 15 to 20 minutes

Baja California is a fishing paradise. To celebrate a good catch, bake swordfish with oil and green onions to bring out its meaty flavor and texture.

- 4 **swordfish steaks**
- 4 **to 6 tablespoons olive oil**
- ½ **cup sliced green onions (including some tops)**
- ¼ **cup chopped parsley**
- 1 **large tomato, seeded and chopped**
  Lime wedges

Place swordfish in a single layer in a baking dish; brush well with oil. Sprinkle with green onions.

Bake, uncovered, in a 350° oven until fish is just slightly translucent or wet inside when cut (15 to 20 minutes). Transfer fish to a serving platter and sprinkle with parsley and tomato. Offer with lime wedges. Makes 4 servings.

Per serving: 375 calories, 41 g protein, 3 g carbohydrates, 22 g total fat, 79 mg cholesterol, 187 mg sodium

Salmon meets its match—a tart, herb-rich cilantro sauce—in this elegant entrée. Serve
Salmon en Salsa Verde (recipe on facing page) with the Mexican noodle specialty called
Sopa Seca de Fideo (recipe on page 93) and sautéed golden and red cherry tomatoes.
Bolillos (recipe on page 105) or French bread complete a memorable dinner.

Vegetables, Beans & Rice

*I*f you are among the many people today who search for tantalizing and healthful alternatives to meat, you need look no further than this chapter. Its mouth-watering recipes for vegetables, beans, and rice are rich in appetizing flavor and color.

*S*ample utterly simple grilled corn, a brisk squash stew, or one of the new ways to stuff chiles on page 95. Get more acquainted with humble dried beans (such as pinto, black, and kidney), a staple in the Mexican diet since ancient times and an excellent source of flavor and protein.

*A*nd discover the broad range of rice and noodle dishes cooked with vegetables and herbs. All of these recipes can stand alone or accompany any main dish.

Elote Asado
GRILLED CORN

Preparation time: About 15 minutes
Cooking time: 20 minutes

On a balmy summer evening, let the fresh flavor of cilantro accent ears of sweet corn as they grill atop the barbecue.

- **6 ears of corn**
- **¼ cup butter or margarine, at room temperature**
- **½ cup firmly packed fresh cilantro (coriander) leaves, chopped**
- **Salt and pepper**
- **1 cup sour cream (optional)**
- **6 ounces grated or crumbled cotija (page 13) or Parmesan cheese**

Gently peel back corn husks but do not tear off. Pull out and discard silk; rinse corn and pat dry.

Cut 6 rectangles of aluminum foil, each 8 inches wide. Rub butter over each cob and sprinkle with cilantro. Season to taste with salt and pepper. Pull husks back over corn and wrap each ear in foil.

Place corn on a grill 4 to 6 inches above a solid bed of medium-hot coals. Cook, turning 2 or 3 times, for 20 minutes. Remove corn and carefully peel off foil; let cool slightly. Peel back husks and spread each ear with sour cream, if desired; sprinkle with cheese. Makes 6 servings.

Per serving: 243 calories, 10 g protein, 18 g carbohydrates, 16 g total fat, 43 mg cholesterol, 586 mg sodium

Rajas con Papas
CHILE STRIPS WITH POTATOES

Preparation time: 10 minutes
Cooking time: About 25 minutes

This robust mix of potatoes and roasted chiles is a favorite quesadilla stuffing that's also delicious with scrambled eggs or roasted meats.

- **Salt**
- **¾ pound red thin-skinned potatoes**
- **4 poblano or Anaheim chiles**
- **¼ cup salad oil**
- **½ cup chopped onion**

In a 4- to 6-quart pan, bring enough salted water to cover potatoes to a rolling boil. Add potatoes and cook until just tender when pierced (15 to 20 minutes). Drain and let cool. Cut potatoes into 1-inch chunks.

Meanwhile, holding chiles with tongs, rotate over a gas flame, one at a time, until charred and blistered (about 2 minutes). Or arrange chiles on a baking sheet and broil 3 inches below heat, rotating often, until charred (about 6 minutes). Seal in a plastic bag and let sweat until cool.

Peel chiles under cool running water. Stem and seed; cut lengthwise into thin strips. Heat oil in a 10- to 12-inch frying pan over medium-high heat. When oil is hot, add onion and chiles and cook, stirring often, for 5 minutes. Add potatoes and continue to cook, stirring, for 5 more minutes. Makes 4 servings.

Per serving: 207 calories, 2 g protein, 19 g carbohydrates, 14 g total fat, 0 mg cholesterol, 9 mg sodium

Batatas con Lima y Tequila TRY
SWEET POTATOES WITH LIME & TEQUILA

Preparation time: About 10 minutes
Cooking time: About 20 minutes

Jazz up ordinary sweet potatoes with Latin flair, and you achieve an extraordinary side dish for barbecued poultry or pork.

- **2 pounds sweet potatoes**
- **¾ cup (¼ lb. plus ¼ cup) butter or margarine**
- **2 tablespoons sugar**
- **2 tablespoons tequila**
- **1 tablespoon lime juice**
- **Salt and pepper**
- **Lime wedges**

Peel sweet potatoes; coarsely shred.

In a 12- to 14-inch frying pan, melt butter over medium heat. Add potatoes and sugar. Cook, turning occasionally, until potatoes begin to caramelize and look slightly translucent (about 15 minutes). Stir in tequila and lime juice and continue to cook for 3 more minutes. Season to taste with salt and pepper.

Offer with lime wedges to squeeze over individual servings. Makes 6 to 8 servings.

Per serving: 251 calories, 2 g protein, 23 g carbohydrates, 17 g total fat, 47 mg cholesterol, 187 mg sodium

Celebrate springtime with a colorful platter of crisp
Esparragos con Tomatillos (recipe on facing page). Serve the stately spears cold under
a confettilike topping of finely diced tomatillos, tomato, and shredded Parmesan,
accented with a squeeze of lemon. As a side dish or first course, it's spectacular.

Esparragos con Tomatillos

ASPARAGUS WITH TOMATILLOS

Pictured on facing page

Preparation time: 15 to 20 minutes
Cooking time: 3 to 5 minutes

In the spring, when asparagus is newly picked, this elegant salad shows off the green spears with vivid tomatoes and tomatillos.

- 1 **pound asparagus**
- 3 **tablespoons olive oil**
- 4 **large tomatillos (about 1½-inch diameter), husked, rinsed, and finely diced**
- 1 **small pear-shaped tomato, cored and finely diced**
- ¼ **cup crumbled cotija (page 13) or finely shredded Parmesan cheese**
  Lemon wedges
  Salt and pepper (optional)

Snap off and discard tough ends of asparagus; rinse spears. Pour water to a depth of 1 inch into a wide frying pan and bring to a boil over high heat. Add asparagus and cook, uncovered, until barely tender when pierced (3 to 5 minutes); drain. Immerse in ice water. When cool, drain again; arrange on a platter or on 4 salad plates.

Mix oil, tomatillos, and tomato; spoon over asparagus. Sprinkle with cheese and garnish with lemon wedges. If desired, season to taste with salt and pepper. Makes 4 servings.

Per serving: 146 calories, 5 g protein, 7 g carbohydrates, 12 g total fat, 4 mg cholesterol, 90 mg sodium

Pudin de Elote

BAKED CORN PUDDING

Preparation time: About 20 minutes
Baking time: About 55 minutes

A great choice for entertaining, this sweet corn pudding can accompany meat or star as a light brunch casserole.

- 6 **tablespoons butter or margarine**
- 1 **large onion, chopped**
- 1 **clove garlic, minced or pressed**
- 1 *each* **medium-size red and green bell peppers, seeded and chopped**
- ⅓ **cup all-purpose flour**
- 1 **teaspoon salt**
- 1 **tablespoon sugar**
- ¼ **teaspoon pepper**
- 2 **cans (about 1 lb.** *each***) cream-style corn**
- 6 **eggs, lightly beaten**
- 2 **cups milk**

In a 5-quart pan, melt butter over medium heat. Add onion, garlic, and bell peppers. Cook, stirring often, until onion is soft (about 5 minutes). Stir in flour, salt, sugar, and pepper; cook, stirring, until bubbly. Remove from heat. Add corn, eggs, and milk, stirring until mixture is well blended.

Pour corn mixture into a buttered shallow 3-quart baking dish.

Bake, uncovered, in a 350° oven until center appears set when dish is gently shaken (about 55 minutes). Makes 10 servings.

Per serving: 233 calories, 8 g protein, 26 g carbohydrates, 12 g total fat, 190 mg cholesterol, 615 mg sodium

Guisado de Chayote

STEWED CHAYOTE SQUASH

Preparation time: 15 minutes
Cooking time: About 25 minutes

Similar in taste to zucchini, the Mexican squash known as *chayote* is also called mirliton in some stateside markets.

- 1 **pound chayote squash or zucchini**
- 2 **tablespoons salad oil**
- 1 **medium-size onion, chopped**
- 2 **cloves garlic, thinly sliced**
- 1 **large tomato, seeded and chopped**
- 1 **canned chipotle chile in adobe sauce, mashed (optional)**
- ⅓ **cup sour cream**
- 4 **ounces grated or crumbled cotija (page 13) or Parmesan cheese**

Peel and pit chayote; cut into small chunks.

Heat oil in a 10- to 12-inch frying pan over medium-high heat. When oil is hot, add onion and garlic; cook, stirring often, until onion is soft (about 5 minutes). Add squash, tomato, and, if desired, chile; stir well. Reduce heat, cover, and simmer, stirring occasionally, until squash is tender (about 20 minutes). Remove from heat and stir in sour cream. Sprinkle each serving with cheese. Makes 4 servings.

Per serving: 241 calories, 9 g protein, 11 g carbohydrates, 19 g total fat, 31 mg cholesterol, 512 mg sodium

Calabacita con Elote

ZUCCHINI WITH CORN & PEPPERS

Preparation time: About 15 minutes
Cooking time: About 5 minutes

A colorful companion to any main dish, *calabacita con elote* combines three of Mexico's time-honored staples: squash, corn, and peppers. A quick sauté keeps the vegetables bright and crisp.

- 3 tablespoons butter or margarine
- 2½ pounds zucchini, thinly sliced
  About 1½ cups fresh or frozen, thawed corn kernels
- 1 red bell pepper, seeded and diced
- 1 medium-size onion, chopped
- 2 cloves garlic, minced or pressed
  Salt and pepper

In a wide frying pan, melt butter over high heat. Add zucchini, corn, bell pepper, onion, and garlic. Cook, stirring, until vegetables are tender-crisp (about 5 minutes). Season to taste with salt and pepper. Makes 8 to 10 servings.

Per serving: 72 calories, 2 g protein, 9 g carbohydrates, 4 g total fat, 9 mg cholesterol, 43 mg sodium

Ejotes con Limon

LEMON GREEN BEANS

Preparation time: About 10 minutes
Cooking time: About 7 minutes

The cooks of Guadalajara prepare green beans with a simple parsley-butter sauce, finished with a typical Mexican flourish—fresh lemon juice.

- 1½ pounds green beans
  Salt
- 3 tablespoons butter or margarine, melted
- ¼ teaspoon pepper
- 1 tablespoon minced parsley
- 3 tablespoons fresh lemon juice
  Salt

Trim stem ends of green beans; cut beans into 1½-inch lengths.

In a 3- to 4-quart pan, cook beans, uncovered, in boiling salted water just until tender-crisp (about 7 minutes). Drain; transfer to a serving dish.

In a small bowl, mix butter, pepper, parsley, and lemon juice; pour over beans and toss well. Season to taste with salt. Makes 6 servings.

Per serving: 84 calories, 2 g protein, 8 g carbohydrates, 6 g total fat, 16 mg cholesterol, 65 mg sodium

Chili Verde

GREEN CHILI

Pictured on page 67

Preparation time: 30 minutes
Cooking time: About 45 minutes

Don't be surprised to find this chili in the vegetable chapter—it's full of vegetables but contains neither beans nor meat. Cheese adds protein and makes the chili filling.

- 4 large onions, sliced
- 2 cloves garlic, minced or pressed
- ¼ cup salad oil
- 4 large green bell peppers, stemmed, halved, and seeded
- 2 large cans (7 oz. *each*) whole green chiles, split lengthwise
- 1 tablespoon dry oregano leaves
- 2 cans (13 oz. *each*) tomatillos
- 6 cups regular-strength chicken broth
- 4 fresh jalapeño chiles, stemmed, seeded, and chopped
- ½ cup chopped fresh cilantro (coriander)
- 2 cups (8 oz.) shredded jalapeño jack cheese
  Sour cream or plain yogurt

In a 6- to 8-quart pan combine onions, garlic, and oil over medium heat. Cook, stirring often, until onions are very soft and golden (about 30 minutes). Meanwhile, thinly slice bell peppers and green chiles crosswise.

Add oregano, tomatillos and their liquid, broth, bell peppers, green chiles, and jalapeño chiles to pan. Bring to a boil; reduce heat, cover, and simmer until bell peppers are very tender, about 15 minutes. (At this point, you may cool, cover, and refrigerate for up to 2 days; reheat before continuing.)

Stir in cilantro. Ladle chili into individual bowls, sprinkle with cheese, and top with a dollop of sour cream. Makes 8 servings.

Per serving: 236 calories, 9 g protein, 17 g carbohydrates, 16 g total fat, 30 mg cholesterol, 572 mg sodium

Frijoles de Olla

POT BEANS

Preparation time: 5 minutes, plus at least 12 hours to soak beans
Cooking time: About 2½ hours

Slow simmering in a ceramic pot, or *olla*, gives this Mexican staple its name (you can use a metal pan). Traditionally cooked with lard to add richness, here the beans are simmered in broth instead.

- 2½ **cups (about 1 lb.) dried pinto beans, sorted of debris**
- 4 **cups regular-strength chicken broth**
- 1 **medium-size onion, chopped**
  Salt

Rinse beans and place in a large bowl. Cover with cold water and soak at room temperature for at least 12 hours. Drain.

Place beans, broth, and onion in a 4-quart pan. Bring to a boil; reduce heat, partially cover pan, and simmer until beans are tender (about 2½ hours). Season to taste with salt. Makes 6 to 8 servings.

Per serving: 213 calories, 13 g protein, 38 g carbohydrates, 2 g total fat, 0 mg cholesterol, 508 mg sodium

Frijoles Negros

BLACK BEANS ✓

Preparation time: About 15 minutes
Cooking time: 2 to 2½ hours

Once considered a Latin American specialty, black beans have become familiar across much of the United States. Mexican cooks insist that adding *epazote* (page 15) to the pot will ease digestion (proper cooking should do the same).

Versatile black beans can be mashed and refried (recipe at right), or enjoyed for their full flavor cooked simply, as in this recipe.

- ½ **pound salt pork**
- 1 **large onion, chopped**
- 2 **cloves garlic, minced or pressed**
- 2½ **cups (about 1 lb.) dried black beans**
- 1 **teaspoon crumbled dry epazote leaves (optional)**
- 5 **cups water**
- 4 **cups regular-strength beef or chicken broth**
  Salt

In a 4- to 5-quart pan, cook pork over medium-high heat until fat begins to melt. Add onion and garlic and cook, stirring often, until onion is soft (about 5 minutes).

Sort beans and discard debris; rinse well. Add to pan with epazote, if desired; pour in water and broth. Bring to a boil over high heat; reduce heat, cover, and simmer until beans are tender (2 to 2½ hours). If beans are too soupy, uncover and bring to a boil over medium-high heat. Cook, stirring often, until thickened. Season to taste with salt. Makes 6 to 8 servings.

Per serving: 425 calories, 15 g protein, 38 g carbohydrates, 24 g total fat, 24 mg cholesterol, 820 mg sodium

Frijoles Refritos

REFRIED BEANS

Preparation time: 10 minutes, plus at least 12 hours to soak beans
Cooking time: About 2¾ hours

Though the name suggests that it means "fried again," *refrito* actually means "very well fried." The secret of this Mexican classic is to use ample fat, for which we offer a range of choices; bacon drippings give the most flavor.

- 2½ **cups (about 1 lb.) dried pinto or black beans, sorted of debris**
- 1 **medium-size onion, diced**
- ½ **cup hot bacon drippings or melted butter, margarine, or lard**
  Salt

Rinse beans and place in a large bowl. Cover with cold water and soak at room temperature for at least 12 hours. Drain.

Place beans and onion in a 3-quart pan and add enough water to cover by 1 inch; bring to a boil. Reduce heat, cover, and simmer until beans are very tender and mash easily (about 2½ hours); add water as needed. Drain, reserving 1 cup of the liquid.

With a potato masher or in a blender or food processor, mash (or whirl) beans until coarsely puréed (add some cooking liquid, if necessary). Stir in bacon drippings. Return mixture to pan. Cook, stirring constantly, over medium-high heat until fat is absorbed and beans are very hot (about 10 minutes). Season to taste with salt. Makes 6 to 8 servings.

Per serving: 299 calories, 12 g protein, 37 g carbohydrates, 12 g total fat, 10 mg cholesterol, 77 mg sodium

Frijoles Borrachos

"DRUNKEN" BEANS

Pictured on facing page

Preparation time: 20 minutes, plus at least 12 hours to soak beans
Cooking time: About 2½ hours

A specialty of Monterrey (home to many of Mexico's breweries), these savory beans are cooked with beer; hence, their intoxicating name. Another version, made without beer and known as *frijoles charros* (cowboy beans), is popular on Mexican cattle ranches.

- 2½ **cups (about 1 lb.) dried pinto or kidney beans, sorted of debris**
- 2 **tablespoons salad oil**
- 2 **strips thick-sliced bacon, diced**
- 2 **jalapeño or other small hot chiles, stemmed, seeded, and chopped**
- 1 **large onion, chopped**
- 3 **cloves garlic, minced or pressed**
- 1 **bottle (12 oz.) of beer**
- 2 **cups regular-strength chicken broth or water**
- 1 **large can (8 oz.) tomato sauce**
- 1 **tablespoon dry oregano leaves**
- 2 **teaspoons ground cumin**

Rinse beans and place in a large bowl. Cover with cold water and soak at room temperature for at least 12 hours. Drain.

Heat oil in an 8- to 10-quart pan over medium heat. When oil is hot, add bacon and cook until just lightly browned. Add chiles, onion, and garlic and continue to cook, stirring, until vegetables are soft (about 5 minutes). Add beans, beer, broth, tomato sauce, oregano, and cumin; bring to a boil, stirring. Reduce heat, partially cover pan, and simmer, stirring often, until beans are tender and most of the liquid is absorbed (about 2½ hours). Makes 8 to 10 servings.

Per serving: 260 calories, 12 g protein, 36 g carbohydrates, 8 g total fat, 5 mg cholesterol, 398 mg sodium

COWBOY BEANS

Prepare as directed for **Frijoles Borrachos** (above), but instead of beer, use an additional 1½ cups **regular-strength chicken broth** or water.

Per serving: 260 calories, 12 g protein, 35 g carbohydrates, 9 g total fat, 5 mg cholesterol, 547 mg sodium

Torta de Frijoles con Chorizo

CHORIZO & BEAN SANDWICH

Preparation time: About 1 hour; 15 minutes if using purchased chorizo and salsa
Cooking time: About 20 minutes

Ask for a "torta" in Mexico, and you'll get a meat and bean sandwich on the chewy roll known as a *bolillo* (page 105). In this example, spicy chorizo sausage contrasts with mellow cheese, canned beans, and—for convenience—crisp purchased rolls.

You can also make a torta by substituting bread for the flour tortillas in Basic Burritos (page 28); just spread crispy rolls with Guacamole (page 44), top with meat and garnishes, and serve like a sandwich.

- ⅔ **cup Tomatillo Salsa (page 49) or purchased green chile salsa**
- 4 **rectangular crusty rolls (*each* 6 to 8 inches long)**
- 2 **tablespoons butter or margarine**
- ¾ **pound Chorizo (page 39) or purchased chorizo sausages, casings removed**
- 1 **large onion, sliced**
- 1 **large can (15 oz.) pinto beans, drained**
- ⅓ **cup whipping cream**
- ½ **pound (8 oz.) shredded Cheddar, mozzarella, or Chihuahua cheese (page 13)**

Prepare Tomatillo Salsa; set aside.

Cut rolls in half horizontally; butter cut sides. Place rolls, buttered sides up, on a large baking sheet and broil 6 inches below heat until golden (about 2 minutes).

Prepare Chorizo and crumble into a 10- to 12-inch frying pan over medium heat. Cook, stirring often, until lightly browned (about 10 minutes). Remove with a slotted spoon and set aside.

Discard all but 3 tablespoons of the fat from pan. Add onion and cook, stirring, over medium-high heat until soft and lightly browned (about 7 minutes). Remove from heat and add beans, mashing well; then stir in sausage, cream, and ⅓ cup of the salsa.

Mound equal portions of bean mixture over bottoms of rolls. Sprinkle cheese equally over beans and broil 6 inches below heat until cheese is melted (2 to 3 minutes). Serve with toasted roll tops. Offer remaining ⅓ cup salsa to spoon on sandwiches. Makes 4 servings.

Per serving: 1,003 calories, 41 g protein, 85 g carbohydrates, 55 g total fat, 155 mg cholesterol, 1,825 mg sodium

*Slow-cooking in spices and beer develops the savory richness of
Frijoles Borrachos, or "Drunken" Beans (recipe on facing page), a specialty of northern
Mexico. A traditional accompaniment to almost any Mexican meal, beans also make a
healthful and filling "workingman's lunch" when served alone with frosty beer.*

Arroz a la Mexicana
MEXICAN RICE

Preparation time: About 15 minutes
Cooking time: 35 to 40 minutes

Spicy, tomato-bright rice, a mainstay of Mexico, is also called Spanish rice. It rounds out any casual Mexican meal.

To peel tomatoes, dip into boiling water for 10 seconds; skins will slip off easily.

  4 tablespoons salad oil
  2 tablespoons butter or margarine
  2 cups long-grain rice
  1 large onion, chopped
  2 cloves garlic, minced or pressed
  2 Anaheim chiles, stemmed, seeded, and chopped; or 1 small can (4 oz.) diced green chiles
  ¾ pound tomatoes, peeled, seeded, and chopped
  4 cups regular-strength chicken broth
  ¼ cup firmly packed fresh cilantro (coriander) leaves, chopped

Heat oil and butter in a 4- to 6-quart pan over medium-high heat. When butter is melted, add rice and cook, stirring, until lightly browned (about 3 minutes). Add onion, garlic, and chiles; continue to cook, stirring, for 5 more minutes. Add tomatoes and broth. Bring to a boil; reduce heat, cover, and simmer until liquid is absorbed and rice is tender (25 to 30 minutes). Remove from heat and stir in cilantro. Makes 6 servings.

Per serving: 384 calories, 7 g protein, 56 g carbohydrates, 15 g total fat, 10 mg cholesterol, 717 mg sodium

Arroz Blanco
WHITE RICE

Pictured on page 30

Preparation time: 10 minutes
Cooking time: 30 to 35 minutes

Simple yet elegant, this rice pilaf is considered appropriate for a formal Mexican dinner. But you'll enjoy it any time you wish to serve rice.

  3 tablespoons salad oil
  2 tablespoons butter or margarine
  1 large onion, chopped
  2 cups long-grain rice
  4 cups regular-strength chicken broth or water

Heat oil and butter in a 4-quart pan over medium-high heat. When butter is melted, add onion and cook, stirring, until soft (about 5 minutes). Add rice and stir until coated; add broth and bring to a boil. Reduce heat, cover, and simmer until liquid is absorbed and rice is tender (25 to 30 minutes). Makes 6 servings.

Per serving: 349 calories, 6 g protein, 53 g carbohydrates, 12 g total fat, 10 mg cholesterol, 712 mg sodium

Arroz con Pollo
CHICKEN WITH RICE

Preparation time: About 15 minutes
Cooking time: About 1 hour and 10 minutes

Probably inspired by *paella*, which Spain's conquistadors brought to Mexico, this family-style meal has become a classic in its own right.

  ½ pound diced salt pork
  2 tablespoons olive oil or salad oil
    3- to 3½-pound frying chicken, cut up
  ½ cup chopped onion
  1 clove garlic, minced or pressed
  2 large peeled tomatoes or 1 cup drained canned tomatoes, cut into chunks
  1 cup long-grain rice
    About 2 cups regular-strength chicken broth
  1½ cups fresh or frozen thawed peas
    Salt and pepper

In a wide frying pan, cook salt pork over medium heat until well browned; discard drippings. Set aside.

Add oil to pan and heat. When oil is hot, add chicken, several pieces at a time, and cook until well browned on all sides (about 10 minutes). Repeat for remaining chicken, setting aside as cooked. Discard all but 2 tablespoons of the drippings.

Add onion and garlic and cook, stirring, until onion is soft (about 5 minutes). Stir in tomatoes, rice, browned pork, and 2 cups of the broth. Return chicken to pan; cover and cook over low heat until meat near thighbone is no longer pink when slashed and rice is tender to bite (about 45 minutes); add more broth as needed to prevent sticking. Stir in peas during last few minutes of cooking.

Season to taste with salt and pepper. Makes 4 to 6 servings.

Per serving: 633 calories, 34 g protein, 35 g carbohydrates, 39 g total fat, 108 mg cholesterol, 745 mg sodium

Arroz con Chicaros y Jamon

RICE WITH PEAS & HAM

Preparation time: About 20 minutes
Cooking time: 35 to 45 minutes

A type of *sopa seca*, or dry soup (so-called because all the broth is absorbed), this hearty dish can be served as a separate course or as a side dish.

- 6 **tablespoons butter or margarine**
- 1 **medium-size onion, finely chopped**
- 1 **clove garlic, minced or pressed**
- 2 **carrots, diced**
- 2 **jalapeño or other small hot chiles, stemmed, seeded, and minced**
- ¾ **pound baked ham, diced**
- 2 **cups long-grain rice**
- 1 **cup tomato purée**
- 4 **cups regular-strength chicken broth**
- 1 **cup fresh or frozen thawed peas**

In a wide frying pan, melt butter over medium-high heat. Add onion, garlic, carrots, and jalapeños; cook, stirring, until vegetables are soft (about 5 minutes). Add ham and rice and cook for 2 more minutes. Stir in tomato purée and broth.

Bring mixture to a boil; reduce heat, cover, and simmer until all liquid is absorbed and rice is tender (25 to 35 minutes). Stir in peas. Let stand for 5 minutes. Makes 6 servings.

Per serving: 504 calories, 21 g protein, 63 g carbohydrates, 19 g total fat, 65 mg cholesterol, 1,817 mg sodium

Arroz con Queso

BAKED RICE WITH CHEESE

Preparation time: About 15 minutes
Baking time: About 35 minutes

Chile- and herb-sprinkled rice, baked with cheese and sour cream, provides a superb accompaniment to Yucatecan Leg of Lamb (page 69) or other roasts.

- 8 **cups cooked rice**
- 2 **large cans (7 oz. *each*) diced green chiles**
- ½ **cup *each* firmly packed minced fresh cilantro (coriander) and parsley**
- ¾ **cup minced green onions (including tops)**
- 1½ **cups sour cream**
  Salt and pepper
- 1¾ **cups (7 oz.) shredded jack cheese**

In a large bowl, combine rice, chiles, cilantro, parsley, and green onions. Add sour cream and stir until blended; season to taste with salt and pepper.

Spread half the rice mixture in a 9- by 13-inch baking pan and top with half the cheese; repeat layers. Bake in a 350° oven until hot and bubbly (about 35 minutes). Makes 8 to 10 servings.

Per serving: 330 calories, 9 g protein, 44 g carbohydrates, 13 g total fat, 30 mg cholesterol, 354 mg sodium

Sopa Seca de Fideo

VERMICELLI WITH VEGETABLES

Pictured on page 83

Preparation time: About 15 minutes
Cooking time: About 25 minutes

Sopa seca, like many famous terms in Mexican cuisine, is the down-to-earth description of a magnificent dish. Broth is absorbed by rice or noodles during cooking; serve the "dry soup" as a separate course or as a side dish.

- 8 **ounces coiled vermicelli or spaghettini**
- 2 **tablespoons butter or margarine**
- 3 **tablespoons salad oil**
- 1 **medium-size onion, chopped**
- 2 **cloves garlic, minced or pressed**
- 2 **Anaheim chiles, stemmed, seeded, and chopped; or 1 small can (4 oz.) diced green chiles**
- 3 **large tomatoes (about 1 lb. *total*), peeled, seeded, and chopped**
- 1 **teaspoon dry oregano leaves**
- 1 **cup fresh or frozen thawed peas**
- 2 **cups regular-strength chicken broth**
  Salt and pepper

Place noodles in a plastic bag, arranging in one layer. With a rolling pin, break into small pieces. Set aside.

Heat butter and oil in a 10- to 12-inch frying pan over medium-high heat. When butter is melted, add onion, garlic, and chiles and cook, stirring, until soft (about 5 minutes). Add noodles and stir well; continue to cook, stirring constantly, for 2 more minutes. Add tomatoes, oregano, peas, and broth and bring to a boil. Reduce heat, cover, and simmer until liquid is absorbed (about 15 minutes). Season to taste with salt and pepper. Makes 4 servings.

Per serving: 438 calories, 12 g protein, 58 g carbohydrates, 18 g total fat, 16 mg cholesterol, 699 mg sodium

For a new twist on a classic favorite, char poblanos "au naturel," then stuff to create Grilled Chiles with Shrimp (recipe on facing page). Neither batter nor frying is involved, so you can savor the chile's full intensity. Enjoy as a side dish or light entrée with Tomatillo Salsa (recipe on page 49) and sour cream.

Chiles Rellenos a New Way

Improvise on a classic? It's an unusual approach to Mexican cooking, but we think our variation on the standard chile relleno will meet with even the most traditional cook's approval.

After stuffing fresh, mild chiles, you then bake or grill them "au naturel." The difference? They are lighter than the usual egg-coated and fried version—and the true character of the chile comes through with more authority. Use long, slender Anaheims, stubby poblanos, or any other large chile suitable for stuffing that you can find. Experiment with different types to discover your favorite.

Here are three tempting ways to sample the new chiles rellenos—plumped with a creamy filling and baked; stuffed with tender shrimp, then grilled on the barbecue; or roasted with Cheddar and mozzarella cheese.

Chiles with Creamy Corn Filling

- 12 fresh Anaheim, poblano, or other large mild chiles
- 2 tablespoons butter or margarine
- 1 medium-size onion, finely chopped
- 3½ cups fresh or frozen thawed corn kernels
- 1 teaspoon dry oregano leaves
- 1 cup (about 5 oz.) grated or crumbled cotija (page 13) or Parmesan cheese
- ⅓ cup sour cream
  About 12 ounces jack cheese

Slit chiles lengthwise; pull out and discard seeds. Set aside.

In a 10- to 12-inch frying pan, melt butter over medium-high heat; add onion and cook, stirring, until soft (about 5 minutes). Stir in corn and oregano and continue to cook for 5 more minutes.

Remove from heat and stir in cotija cheese and sour cream. Spoon filling equally into chiles and arrange, cut sides up, in a 10- by 15-inch baking pan. Cut jack cheese into 12 equal strips and stuff a strip into each chile. Bake, uncovered, in a 400° oven until chiles are soft and lightly tinged with brown (about 25 minutes). Makes 12 servings.

Per serving: 233 calories, 12 g protein, 15 g carbohydrates, 15 g total fat, 40 mg cholesterol, 350 mg sodium

Grilled Chiles with Shrimp

Pictured on facing page

Tomatillo Salsa (page 49) or purchased green chile salsa
- 8 to 12 fresh Anaheim, poblano, or other large mild chiles
- 1 pound cooked and peeled small shrimp
- ¾ cup thinly sliced green onions (including tops)
  Fresh cilantro (coriander) sprigs
  Sour cream

Prepare Tomatillo Salsa; cover and refrigerate.

Place chiles on a lightly greased grill 4 to 6 inches above a solid bed of hot coals. Cook, uncovered, until chiles are slightly charred on one side (2 to 3 minutes).

Remove from heat and peel off any skin that comes away easily. Slit each chile lengthwise down cooked side; pull out and discard seeds. Let fire burn down to medium heat.

Mix shrimp and green onions; spoon equally into chiles. Place filled chiles, slit sides up, on grill; cover barbecue. Cook until shrimp mixture is hot to touch (5 to 7 minutes). Tranfer chiles to a plate and garnish with cilantro; offer with salsa and sour cream to spoon over individual servings. Makes 8 to 12 servings.

Per serving: 54 calories, 9 g protein, 4 g carbohydrates, 1 g total fat, 74 mg cholesterol, 88 mg sodium

Roasted Cheese-stuffed Chiles

- 4 fresh Anaheim, poblano, or other large mild chiles
- ½ cup *each* shredded Cheddar and mozzarella cheeses

Leaving stems on, slit chiles lengthwise and discard seeds and ribs. Mix Cheddar and mozzarella and fill chiles equally.

Place chiles, slit sides up, in a 9-inch square baking pan. Bake, uncovered, in a 400° oven until chiles are soft and lightly tinged with brown (about 25 minutes). Makes 4 servings.

Per serving: 120 calories, 8 g protein, 8 g carbohydrates, 8 g total fat, 26 mg cholesterol, 145 mg sodium

Egg Dishes

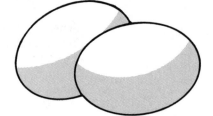

Tired of boring breakfasts? Wake up your palate with a morning meal from Mexico. Inspired by traditional Mexican brunches, the recipes in this chapter feature eggs with tortillas, beans, salsas, cheese—everything but bacon. There's even a chile-laced hollandaise in our potent Eggs Tijuana.

But eggs are too good to limit to breakfast. Many of the dishes on the next pages, such as our Egg & Chile Casserole and *Papa-dzules* (tortillas filled with eggs and pork), provide perfect fare for lunch or dinner. All of these dishes need little more than fruit and beverages to round out an exciting meal.

So, even if you start your day with just coffee and a roll, you'll find plenty of delicious reasons to enjoy Mexican-style eggs later on.

Huevos Rancheros

MEXICAN EGGS WITH TORTILLAS

Preparation time: About 1 hour
Assembly time: About 15 minutes (including time for frying eggs)

Mexicans linger over brunch with true apprecia-tion, and *huevos rancheros* is often the reason. When made with soft-fried tortillas, you can roll them up to eat; with crisp tortillas, use a knife and fork.

> **Salsa Fresca (page 48)**
> **Spiced Tomato Sauce (recipe follows)**
> **Fried Tortillas (directions follow)**
> **Garnishes (suggestions follow)**
> 6 **or 12 fried eggs**

Prepare Salsa Fresca; cover and refrigerate. Pre-pare Spiced Tomato Sauce and Fried Tortillas; keep warm.

For each serving, place 1 or 2 tortillas on a plate; top with 1 or 2 fried eggs and about ½ cup of the tomato sauce. Accompany with garnishes and salsa. Makes 6 servings.

Spiced Tomato Sauce. Mince 2 large **onions;** seed and mince 1 large **green bell pepper.** In a wide frying pan, combine onions, bell pepper, and 3 tablespoons **salad oil;** cook, stirring often, over medium heat, until onions are soft (about 10 min-utes). Add 1 can (14 oz.) **pear-shaped tomatoes** (break up with a spoon) and their liquid, 1 can (14½ oz.) **regular-strength chicken broth,** 1 can (10 oz.) **red chile sauce,** and ½ teaspoon *each* **dry oregano leaves** and **cumin seeds.** Bring to a boil and cook, uncovered, stirring often, until reduced to about 3 cups.

Fried Tortillas. You will need 6 or 12 **corn tortillas** (6-inch diameter). Heat ½ inch **salad oil** in an 8- to 10-inch frying pan over medium-high heat. When oil is hot, add tortillas, 1 at a time.

For soft-fried tortillas, cook, turning once, just until soft (about 10 seconds total). Drain on paper towels.

For crisp-fried tortillas, cook, turning once, until crisp and golden brown (45 to 60 seconds total). Drain on paper towels.

Garnishes. Choose from the following, arranged in separate bowls: sliced **avocado, fresh cilantro (coriander) sprigs, radishes,** shredded **lettuce,** chopped **green onions** (including tops), shredded **jack or Cheddar cheese,** and **lime wedges.**

Per serving (1 egg): 367 calories, 10 g protein, 34 g carbo-hydrates, 22 g total fat, 246 mg cholesterol, 1,190 mg sodium

Huevos a la Tijuana

EGGS TIJUANA

Preparation time: About 2 hours; 35 minutes if using purchased chorizo
Assembly time: About 10 minutes (including time for poaching eggs)

In this Mexican interpretation of eggs Benedict, a flaky tortilla basket cradles crumbled chorizo sausage and a poached egg. As an eye-opening topper, drizzle on chile-bold hollandaise.

> **Chile Hollandaise (recipe follows)**
> 6 **Tortilla Baskets (page 18)**
> 1 **pound Chorizo (page 39) or purchased chorizo sausages, casings removed**
> 6 **eggs**
> 2 **cups finely shredded iceberg lettuce**
> **Fresh cilantro (coriander) sprigs**

Prepare Chile Hollandaise and set aside.

Prepare Tortilla Baskets and keep warm in a 150° oven. If made ahead, reheat as directed.

Prepare Chorizo and crumble into a 10- to 12-inch frying pan; cook, stirring over medium-high heat until well browned (about 10 minutes). Drain on paper towels. Cover and keep warm in oven.

Pour water to a depth of 1½ inches into a 10- to 12-inch frying pan and bring to a boil. Reduce heat until only an occasional bubble pops to surface. Without crowding, break eggs into water. Cook until set to your liking, gently touching yolk to check firmness (3 to 4 minutes for soft yolks and firm whites). Remove eggs and drain.

Place each basket on a plate. Spoon in ⅓ cup of the lettuce and top with some of the sausage, a poached egg, and about 2 tablespoons of the hol-landaise. Garnish with cilantro. Makes 6 servings.

Chile Hollandaise. In a blender, combine 2 tea-spoons **ground chile powder** or chili powder, 1 tablespoon **hot water,** ½ teaspoon **ground cumin,** 2 teaspoons **lemon juice,** and 1 **egg yolk;** whirl until smooth. With blender on high, pour in ½ cup (¼ lb.) hot melted **butter** or margarine in a thin, steady stream.

Serve hot or at room temperature. If made ahead, cover and refrigerate for up to a week. To reheat, bring to room temperature, set container in hot tap water, and stir occasionally until sauce is warm, adding hot water if necessary.

Per serving: 406 calories, 14 g protein, 15 g carbohydrates, 33 g total fat, 382 mg cholesterol, 457 mg sodium

Huevos con Frijoles Negros y Platanos

EGGS WITH BLACK BEANS & PLANTAINS

Pictured on facing page

Preparation time: About 45 minutes
Assembly time: About 15 minutes (including time for frying eggs)

Taste the Caribbean influences in this brunch combination of eggs, black beans, and starchy plantains. Canned black beans can be found in most supermarkets; look for plantains in Latin produce markets.

> Red Chile Purée (page 48)
> Refried Black Beans (recipe follows)
> Fried Plantains (recipe follows)
> 8 fried eggs
> ⅓ cup grated or crumbled cotija (page 13) or Parmesan cheese
> Lime wedges

Prepare Red Chile Purée; set aside. Prepare Refried Black Beans and Fried Plantains.

Spoon beans equally onto 8 warm plates and top each portion with an egg; arrange plantains alongside. Spoon chile purée over eggs; then sprinkle with cheese. Offer lime wedges to squeeze over individual servings. Makes 8 servings.

Refried Black Beans. In a 4-quart pan, cook 12 slices (about ¾ lb.) **bacon,** diced, over medium-high heat until fat is melted. Add 1 large **onion,** chopped, and cook, stirring, until soft (about 5 minutes).

Drain 4 cans (about 1 lb. *each*) **black beans,** reserving about ½ cup of the liquid. Mash beans with a heavy spoon or potato masher and add to pan. Cook over low heat, stirring often, until hot, moistening mixture with reserved bean liquid as necessary. Season to taste with **salt.** Keep warm.

Fried Plantains. Peel 3 large **plantains** (skins should be almost black) or 4 large, firm, green-tipped bananas. Cut into ¼-inch-thick diagonal slices; set aside.

Pour **salad oil** to a depth of 1 inch into a wide frying pan and heat to 375°F on a deep-frying thermometer. Drop plantain slices, several at a time, into hot oil and cook, turning as needed, until golden brown (2 to 3 minutes).

Meanwhile, line a baking sheet with paper towels. With a slotted spoon, transfer cooked plantains to baking sheet; keep warm in a 150° oven.

Per serving: 737 calories, 25 g protein, 66 g carbohydrates, 43 g total fat, 277 mg cholesterol, 1,368 mg sodium

Papa-dzules

EGG & PORK TORTILLAS

Preparation time: About 40 minutes
Baking time: 20 to 25 minutes

A pumpkin seed sauce flavors this enchiladalike dish. Enjoy it for breakfast or dinner.

> 2¼ cups Pipian Paste (page 79)
> 2 cups regular-strength chicken broth
> 1 pound ground pork
> 8 hard-cooked eggs, peeled and chopped
> 12 flour tortillas (7- to 9-inch diameter)
> 2 tablespoons melted butter or margarine
> Tomato Sauce (recipe follows)
> Fresh cilantro (coriander) sprigs

Prepare Pipian Paste. Combine paste and broth in a 2- to 3-quart pan; stir to blend smoothly. Bring mixture to a boil, stirring, and keep warm. Crumble pork into a 10- to 12-inch frying pan and cook, stirring, over medium heat until browned and crumbly (about 10 minutes). Remove from heat and drain off fat; stir in eggs and 1½ cups of the pipian sauce.

Spoon pork mixture equally down center of each tortilla; roll to enclose filling. Place tortillas, seam sides down, in a 9- by 13-inch baking dish; brush with butter and drizzle with remaining pipian sauce. Cover and bake in a 350° oven until hot (20 to 25 minutes).

Meanwhile, prepare Tomato Sauce. To serve, drizzle tortillas with sauce. Garnish with cilantro. Makes 6 to 8 servings.

Tomato Sauce. Heat 2 tablespoons **salad oil** in a 10- to 12-inch frying pan over medium-high heat. When oil is hot, add 1 large **onion,** chopped; 2 cloves **garlic,** minced or pressed; and 2 or 3 fresh or canned **jalapeño or serrano chiles,** stemmed, seeded, and chopped. Cook, stirring often, for 3 minutes. Add 1 large can (28 oz.) **tomatoes** (break up with a spoon) and their liquid. Cook, stirring, until sauce is thickened (10 to 15 minutes). Season to taste with **salt** and **pepper.**

Per serving: 626 calories, 29 g protein, 49 g carbohydrates, 36 g total fat, 320 mg cholesterol, 1,196 mg sodium

*For a bold start to the day, enjoy a Latin breakfast of Huevos con
Frijoles Negros y Platanos (recipe on facing page), as well as fresh orange juice and
Mexican pastries. You can make the chile purée ahead of time; the beans
and plantains are quick to prepare just before serving.*

Huevos con Queso
MEXICAN EGGS WITH CHEESE

Preparation time: About 25 minutes
Cooking time: About 20 minutes

Reminiscent of *chile con queso* (melted cheese with chiles), cheese sauce is blended with eggs and spooned over tortillas for this filling entrée. Serve with sliced tomatoes and beer or iced tea.

       Tortilla Strips (recipe follows)
   3   tablespoons butter or margarine
   1   small onion, minced
   ½   teaspoon ground cumin
   1   tablespoon all-purpose flour
   ½   cup sour cream
   1½ cups (6 oz.) *each* shredded jack and Cheddar cheeses
   6   eggs, lightly beaten
   ½   cup diced tomatoes
   1   large tomatillo, husked, rinsed, and chopped (optional)
   1   large Anaheim or other mild green chile, stemmed, seeded, and chopped

Prepare Tortilla Strips. Distribute evenly among 6 dinner plates and keep warm in a 150° oven.

In a 10- to 12-inch frying pan, melt butter over low heat. Add onion and cumin; cook, stirring occasionally, until onion is soft (about 5 minutes). Mix in flour; cook, stirring, until bubbly. Remove from heat and blend in sour cream. Return to heat and cook, stirring, over low heat until smooth and bubbly. Add jack and Cheddar cheeses and continue to cook, stirring, until melted. Stir in eggs; cook until eggs are lightly set and mixture looks like soft scrambled eggs (about 10 more minutes).

Dividing equally, spoon egg mixture over tortilla strips and sprinkle with tomatoes, tomatillo, if desired, and chile. Makes 6 servings.

Tortilla Strips. Stack 16 to 18 **corn tortillas** (6-inch diameter) and cut into ¼-inch-wide strips.

Pour **salad oil** to a depth of 1 inch into a 3- to 4-quart pan and heat to 375°F on a deep-frying thermometer. Add strips, a handful at a time, and cook, stirring often, until crisp and lightly browned (about 1 minute). Lift out; drain on paper towels. Sprinkle with **salt.**

Per serving: 747 calories, 26 g protein, 41 g carbohydrates, 53 g total fat, 353 mg cholesterol, 470 mg sodium

Huevos al Horno
MEXICAN EGG CUSTARD

Preparation time: About 20 minutes
Baking time: About 30 minutes

There's no last minute fuss when you bake eggs, and this chile-and-cheese custard is a tempting reason to do so. Offer salsa to season each portion.

       Salsa Fresca (page 48) or purchased salsa
   2   large cans (7 oz. *each*) whole green chiles, split and seeded
   2   cups (8 oz.) *each* shredded Cheddar and jack cheeses
       Pepper
   3   eggs
   1   cup sour cream
   1   medium-size tomato, cored and diced

Prepare Salsa Fresca; set aside.

Arrange half the chiles, spread open, in a single layer in a shallow 2½- to 3-quart baking dish. Evenly sprinkle half the cheese over chiles and lightly sprinkle with pepper; repeat layers.

In a bowl, beat eggs and sour cream until blended. Pour over chiles and cheese. Bake in a 350° oven until custard jiggles only slightly in center when gently shaken and edges begin to brown (about 30 minutes). Let cool for 5 to 10 minutes.

Arrange tomato around edges of dish. Offer salsa to spoon over individual servings. Makes 8 servings.

Per serving: 326 calories, 18 g protein, 6 g carbohydrates, 26 g total fat, 170 mg cholesterol, 673 mg sodium

Cazuela de Huevos con Chiles
EGG & CHILE CASSEROLE

Preparation time: About 20 minutes
Baking time: About 40 minutes

Puffy as a soufflé, yet easy to make, this casserole resembles baked *chiles rellenos* (stuffed chiles).

   2 or 3 large cans (7 oz. *each*) whole green chiles, seeded
   4   corn tortillas (6-inch diameter), cut into wide strips
   4   cups (1 lb.) shredded jack cheese
   1   large tomato, seeded and sliced

8 eggs
½ cup milk
½ teaspoon *each* salt, pepper, ground cumin, and garlic powder
¼ teaspoon onion salt
Paprika

Lay half the chiles in a well-greased 9-inch square baking dish. Top with half the tortilla strips and half the cheese. Arrange tomato slices on top. Repeat layers, using remaining chiles, tortillas, and cheese.

Beat eggs with milk, salt, pepper, cumin, garlic powder, and onion salt; pour over tortilla mixture and sprinkle with paprika.

Bake, uncovered, in a 350° oven until puffy and set in center when lightly touched (about 40 minutes). Let stand for about 10 minutes; cut into squares. Makes 6 to 8 servings.

Per serving: 352 calories, 22 g protein, 13 g carbohydrates, 24 g total fat, 326 mg cholesterol, 873 mg sodium

Huevos con Salsa de Aguacates

EGGS WITH AVOCADO SAUCE

Preparation time: About 10 minutes
Cooking time: About 25 minutes

Cloak hot hard-cooked eggs in a creamy avocado sauce for a delightfully uncomplicated breakfast. Serve with fried patties of *Chorizo* (page 39).

8 eggs
2 tablespoons butter or margarine
2 tablespoons minced onion
1 canned whole green chile, seeded and chopped
1 tablespoon all-purpose flour
½ cup milk
2 avocados, pitted, peeled, and cut into chunks
Salt

Place eggs in a single layer in a wide pan and cover with cold tap water. Bring just to a boil; reduce heat and simmer for 15 minutes. Drain; peel eggs under cold running water and place in a bowl of hot water.

In a small pan, melt butter over medium heat. Add onion and cook, stirring, until soft (about 5 minutes). Add chile, flour, and milk. Cook, stirring, until thickened (about 5 more minutes). In a blender or food processor, whirl avocados until smooth; stir into hot sauce. Season to taste with salt.

Drain eggs, cut in half lengthwise, and arrange on a platter; pour hot sauce over eggs. Makes 4 servings.

Per serving: 399 calories, 15 g protein, 12 g carbohydrates, 33 g total fat, 568 mg cholesterol, 245 mg sodium

Tortillas de Huevos Maya

MAYAN EGG TORTILLAS

Preparation time: About 20 minutes
Cooking time: About 15 minutes

Unsalted pumpkin seeds, or *pepitas* (page 15), enrich the sauce for these egg-filled tortillas.

8 flour tortillas (7- to 9-inch diameter)
½ pound hulled, unsalted pumpkin seeds
½ cup regular-strength chicken broth
3 tablespoons lemon juice
1 clove garlic, peeled
3 tablespoons canned diced green chiles
1 teaspoon pepper
1 cup whipping cream
Salt
10 eggs
3 tablespoons water
2 tablespoons butter or margarine
⅓ cup chopped green onions (including tops)

Wrap tortillas in foil and warm in a 350° oven until hot (about 15 minutes).

Meanwhile, place half the pumpkin seeds in a blender or food processor. Whirl until coarsely chopped. Add broth, lemon juice, garlic, chiles, and pepper; whirl until well blended. Add cream and season to taste with salt; whirl briefly to mix. With a knife, coarsely chop remaining pumpkin seeds and stir into cream mixture; set aside.

Beat eggs with water. In a 10- to 12-inch frying pan, melt butter over medium-low heat. Pour in egg mixture and scramble until barely set and still moist on top.

Dividing equally, spoon eggs down center of each tortilla, top with 2 tablespoons of the cream sauce, and roll to enclose. Arrange, seam sides down, in a 9- by 13-inch baking pan. Spoon remaining sauce over top.

Broil 4 to 6 inches below heat until sauce is lightly browned and mixture is heated through (4 to 6 minutes). Sprinkle with green onions. Makes 4 servings (2 tortillas each).

Per serving: 917 calories, 34 g protein, 84 g carbohydrates, 50 g total fat, 767 mg cholesterol, 847 mg sodium

Cooked cactus strips, called nopalitos, add tart and crunchy excitement to these simple recipes—vivid Three-color Cactus Salad of onions, tomatoes, and cilantro and hearty Chorizo Soup with Cactus (recipes on facing page). If desired, top soup with sour cream for contrast; keep the salad light with just a squeeze of fresh lime.

Edible Cactus

Don't let the thorny skin of *nopales* scare you away—those pads of prickly pear cactus are actually edible. When despined and cooked, they are eaten as a tart and crunchy vegetable.

In spring, look for fresh nopales in Mexican markets. Select firm, blemish-free pads. Remove spines (as directed below) for cooking. Peeling the pads is optional, but always rinse them in cold water after cooking to remove the sticky liquid that is secreted.

Nopalitos, or cut-up nopales, are also available in Mexican markets in 15-ounce jars. They can be used interchangeably with cooked fresh nopales.

Chorizo Soup with Cactus

Pictured on facing page

    Cooked Nopalitos (directions follow) or 1 jar (15 oz.) nopalitos, drained and rinsed

1 pound chorizo sausages, sliced

1 medium-size onion, chopped

1 Anaheim chile, stemmed, seeded, and chopped

1 quart regular-strength chicken broth

½ cup *each* sour cream and diced tomatoes

¼ cup fresh cilantro (coriander) leaves

Prepare Cooked Nopalitos; set aside.

Place sausages in a 4- to 5-quart pan over medium-high heat. Cook, stirring, until browned. Discard all but 1 tablespoon of the fat. Add onion and chile and cook, stirring, until soft (about 5 minutes). Add broth and nopalitos. Bring to a boil; reduce heat, cover, and simmer for 10 minutes. Offer sour cream, tomatoes, and cilantro to spoon over individual servings. Makes 4 servings.

Cooked Nopalitos. Holding pads with a towel to protect your hands, shave spines off 1 pound **fresh nopales** (cactus pads). Trim around pad to remove thorny edge; peel pads, if desired. Slice crosswise into ¼-inch-wide strips.

In a 3- to 4-quart pan, bring 1½ quarts **water** to a boil; add cactus and 1 stemmed and seeded **jalapeño or serrano chile.** Cook, uncovered, over high heat until cactus is tender (5 to 7 minutes). Drain;

rinse with cold water. If made ahead, cover and refrigerate for up to 4 days. Makes about 2 cups.

Per serving: 314 calories, 15 g protein, 14 g carbohydrates, 23 g total fat, 57 mg cholesterol, 1,250 mg sodium

Three-Color Cactus Salad

Pictured on facing page

2 cups Cooked Nopalitos (at left) or 1 jar (15 oz.) nopalitos, drained and rinsed

4 medium-size ripe tomatoes, cored and sliced ¼ inch thick

1 medium-size onion, sliced thinly and separated into rings

    Fresh cilantro (coriander) sprigs

2 limes, *each* cut into 6 wedges

Prepare Cooked Nopalitos. On a large platter, arrange nopalitos, tomatoes, and onion. Garnish with cilantro. Offer limes to squeeze over individual servings. Makes 6 to 8 servings.

Per serving: 32 calories, 1 g protein, 8 g carbohydrates, .16 g total fat, 0 mg cholesterol, 6 mg sodium

Eggs with Cactus Strips

2 cups Cooked Nopalitos (at left) or 1 jar (15 oz.) nopalitos, drained and rinsed

    Salsa Fresca (page 48) or purchased salsa

6 flour tortillas (7- to 9-inch diameter)

2 cups (8 oz.) shredded Cheddar cheese

2 cups chopped tomatoes

6 poached eggs

Prepare Cooked Nopalitos and Salsa Fresca; set aside.

Place tortillas directly on center rack of a 350° oven and bake until crisp and lightly browned (6 to 8 minutes). Remove from oven and place on baking sheets; sprinkle with cheese, nopalitos, and tomatoes. Return to oven and bake until cheese is melted (5 more minutes). Place an egg on top of each tortilla. Offer salsa to spoon over individual servings. Makes 6 servings.

Per serving: 372 calories, 20 g protein, 31 g carbohydrates, 19 g total fat, 314 mg cholesterol, 517 mg sodium

Breads & Pastries

To explore the art of Mexican bakers is to excite your eyes as well as your palate. No creation, simple or grand, is left unadorned. Even the humble *bolillo* has a distinctive oblong shape and slashed top. Ubiquitous *pan dulce* appears as seashells, horns, or ears of corn. And carnival bread brandishes a personal baked-on greeting.

The flavors of Mexican baked goods are as creative as the shapes. Chile, corn, and chorizo give bold character to basic breads; pastries are anointed with honey or powdered sugar. Mexican chocolate, explored in a special feature in this chapter, is unique for its almond-cinnamon accent.

Enjoy the festive look and taste of these breads and pastries as you sample the recipes that follow. But never mind fussy appearances: the more "handcrafted" looking, the better.

Sopaipillas

PUFFY FRIED BREAD

Pictured on page 126

Preparation time: About 40 minutes
Rising time: About 1 hour
Cooking time: About 25 minutes

Since they've crossed the border, these airy pillows of fried bread have become an institution in New Mexico. Serve warm with honey.

- 1 package active dry yeast
- ¼ cup warm water (about 110°F)
- 1½ cups milk
- 3 tablespoons lard or vegetable shortening
- 1 teaspoon salt
- 2 tablespoons sugar
- 1 cup whole wheat flour
- About 4 cups all-purpose flour
- Salad oil
- Powdered sugar

In a large bowl, stir yeast into warm water and let stand until softened (about 5 minutes).

In a 1½- to 2-quart pan, combine milk, lard, salt, and sugar; heat over low heat to 110°F and stir into yeast mixture. Beat in whole wheat flour and 3 cups of the all-purpose flour until dough is stretchy. Knead on a lightly floured board until dough is smooth and satiny, adding more all-purpose flour as needed. Place in a greased bowl; turn to grease top. Cover and let rise at room temperature until doubled (about 1 hour).

Punch dough down; knead briefly. On a lightly floured board, roll dough, a quarter at a time, into rectangles about ⅛ inch thick. Cut each rectangle into 6 equal pieces; place in lightly floured pans and cover with plastic wrap.

Pour oil to a depth of 2 inches into a deep 3- to 4-quart pan and heat to 350°F on a deep-frying thermometer. Add dough, 2 or 3 pieces at a time, and cook, turning and gently pushing bubbly portion into hot oil to help sopaipilla puff evenly, until golden (1 to 2 minutes total). Drain on paper towels. Dust warm sopaipillas with powdered sugar.

If made ahead, let cool, cover, and refrigerate for up to 2 days; freeze for longer storage. To reheat, thaw if frozen. Arrange on baking sheets and bake in a 300° oven, turning once, until warm (5 to 8 minutes). Makes 2 dozen sopaipillas.

Per sopaipilla: 172 calories, 4 g protein, 24 g carbohydrates, 7 g total fat, 4 mg cholesterol, 101 mg sodium

Bolillos

HARD ROLLS

Pictured on page 83

Preparation time: About 30 minutes
Rising time: About 2 hours
Baking time: 35 to 40 minutes

It's not by coincidence that these rolls, crusty on the outside and soft within, closely resemble French bread. They were developed in the 19th century when Mexico was briefly under French dominion.

Serve *bolillos* as you would bread, with dinner, with jam for breakfast, or split and filled as a *torta* (page 90).

- 2 cups water
- 1½ tablespoons sugar
- 1 tablespoon salt
- 2 tablespoons butter or margarine
- 1 package active dry yeast
- About 6 cups all-purpose flour
- 1 teaspoon cornstarch dissolved in ½ cup water

In a small pan, combine water, sugar, salt, and butter; heat over low heat to 110°F. Pour into a large bowl and stir in yeast; let stand until softened (about 5 minutes).

Beat in 5 cups of the flour until incorporated. Knead on a floured board until dough is smooth and elastic (about 10 minutes), adding more flour as needed. Place in a greased bowl; turn to grease top. Cover and let rise in a warm place until doubled (about 1½ hours).

Punch dough down and knead briefly on a lightly floured board. Divide into 16 equal pieces. Form each piece into a smooth ball; then, by rolling and gently pulling from center to ends, shape into an oblong about 4 inches long (center should be thicker than ends). Place rolls 2 inches apart on greased baking sheets. Cover with a kitchen towel and let rise until almost doubled (about 35 minutes).

In a pan, bring cornstarch mixture to a boil; let cool slightly. Brush each roll with mixture. With a sharp knife or razor blade, cut a lengthwise slash, about ¾ inch deep and 2 inches long, into top of each roll.

Bake in a 375° oven until rolls are golden brown and sound hollow when tapped on bottom (35 to 40 minutes). Let cool on a rack; wrap airtight to store. Makes 16 rolls.

Per roll: 190 calories, 5 g protein, 37 g carbohydrates, 2 g total fat, 4 mg cholesterol, 428 mg sodium

Pan de Chiles Verdes
GREEN CHILE BREAD

Pictured on facing page

Preparation time: About 30 minutes
Rising time: About 2½ hours
Baking time: About 40 minutes

A subtle hint of chile adds interest to this yeast bread. Dip cubes into *Chile con Queso* (page 44) or toast slices to serve with poached eggs.

    1   large can (7 oz.) diced green chiles
    ⅛   to ¼ teaspoon ground red pepper (cayenne),
        optional
    1   package active dry yeast
    ¼   cup warm water (about 110°F)
    ½   cup milk
    2   tablespoons butter or margarine
    1   teaspoon salt
    1   tablespoon sugar
        About 4½ cups all-purpose flour

In a blender or food processor, whirl chiles until smoothly puréed. If desired, add ground red pepper. Set aside.

In a large bowl, sprinkle yeast over warm water and let stand until softened (about 5 minutes). Meanwhile, in a small pan, combine milk and butter; heat over low heat to 110°F (butter need not melt completely). Add to yeast mixture along with salt, sugar, chile purée, and 1½ cups of the flour. Stir until thoroughly moistened.

Stir in 1½ more cups of the flour until moistened. With a heavy spoon, beat dough vigorously until stretchy (about 10 minutes). Knead on a floured board until dough is smooth and elastic (about 10 minutes), adding more flour as needed. Place in a greased bowl; turn to grease top. Cover with plastic wrap and let rise in a warm place until doubled (about 1½ hours).

Punch dough down and knead briefly. Shape into a smooth loaf and place in a greased 5- by 9-inch loaf pan. Cover loosely with plastic wrap and let rise in a warm place until dough reaches about an inch above pan rim (about 1 hour).

Bake, uncovered, in a 375° oven until golden brown (about 40 minutes). Transfer to a rack and let cool. Makes 12 to 14 slices (1 loaf).

Per slice: 158 calories, 4 g protein, 30 g carbohydrates, 2 g total fat, 6 mg cholesterol, 266 mg sodium

Pan de Muertos
BREAD OF THE DEAD

Preparation time: About 30 minutes
Rising time: About 2 hours
Baking time: About 35 minutes

Day of the Dead (November 2) may sound like a gruesome holiday, but it's celebrated with much merriment in Mexico. This simple yeast bread featuring crossed "bones" on the surface is traditionally served. It's fun to bake for our own Halloween.

    ¼   cup milk
    ¼   cup plus 2 teaspoons sugar
    ¼   cup butter or margarine, cut into small pieces
    ½   teaspoon salt
    1   package active dry yeast
    ¼   cup warm water (about 110°F)
    2   eggs
        About 3 cups all-purpose flour
    ¼   teaspoon ground cinnamon

In a small pan, scald milk over medium-high heat; remove from heat and stir in ¼ cup of the sugar, butter, and salt. Let cool.

In large bowl of an electric mixer, stir yeast into warm water and let stand until softened (about 5 minutes). Add milk mixture. Separate 1 egg; add yolk to yeast mixture (reserve white). Add remaining egg and 2⅓ cups of the flour; beat until well blended.

Knead on a well-floured board until dough is smooth and velvety (about 10 minutes), adding more flour as needed. Place in a greased bowl; turn to grease top. Cover and let rise in a warm place until doubled (about 1½ hours). Punch dough down and knead briefly.

Cut off ½ cup of the dough; wrap in plastic and set aside. Divide remaining dough into 3 equal parts; shape each into a rope about 12 inches long. Braid ropes, pressing ends to hold securely; place on a greased baking sheet and join ends to make a small wreath. Divide reserved dough in half; shape each portion into a bone. Cross bones and place across wreath.

Cover lightly and let rise in a warm place until puffy (about 30 minutes). Lightly beat reserved egg white and brush over bread. Mix cinnamon and remaining 2 teaspoons sugar; sprinkle over loaf, avoiding bones. Bake in a 350° oven until richly browned (about 35 minutes). Cut into wedges and serve warm. Makes 8 to 10 slices (1 loaf).

Per slice: 221 calories, 6 g protein, 35 g carbohydrates, 6 g total fat, 68 mg cholesterol, 174 mg sodium

*For a wide-awake breakfast, offer sausage-studded Pan de Chorizo (recipe on page 108)
or mildly piquant Pan de Chiles Verdes (recipe on facing page), sliced, toasted,
and served with eggs. Or simply spread with butter to enjoy any time of day. Cubes of
the chile bread make delectable dippers for Chile con Queso, too (recipe on page 44).*

Pan de Chorizo

CHORIZO BREAD

Pictured on page 107

Preparation time: About 15 minutes
Baking time: About 55 minutes

The hearty surprise in this quick bread is fully cooked dry chorizo, found in Latin markets; if it's unavailable, substitute pepperoni.

- 5½ ounces dry chorizo or pepperoni sausages
- 3 cups all-purpose flour
- 3 tablespoons grated Parmesan cheese
- 2 tablespoons firmly packed brown sugar
- 4½ teaspoons baking powder
- 1 teaspoon fennel or caraway seeds
- ½ teaspoon salt
- ¼ teaspoon baking soda
- 1 *each* large package (8 oz.) and small package (3 oz.) cream cheese, softened
- 1 cup milk
- 2 eggs
- ¼ cup butter or margarine, melted

If necessary, remove sausage casings. Coarsely chop sausages. Set aside. In a large bowl, combine flour, Parmesan cheese, sugar, baking powder, fennel seeds, salt, and baking soda.

In another bowl, beat cream cheese until smooth; stir in milk. Beat in eggs, one at a time. Stir in butter and sausages. Add to flour mixture, stirring just to moisten. Spoon batter into a greased 5- by 9-inch loaf pan. Bake in a 375° oven until well browned (about 55 minutes). Let cool on a rack for 5 minutes.

If made ahead, let cool completely, wrap airtight, and store at room temperature for up to a day; freeze for longer storage, thawing wrapped. Reheat, uncovered, in a 350° oven until warm (about 15 minutes). Makes 10 to 12 slices (1 loaf).

Per slice: 344 calories, 10 g protein, 28 g carbohydrates, 21 g total fat, 99 mg cholesterol, 695 mg sodium

Pan de Maiz

CORNBREAD

Preparation time: About 10 minutes
Baking time: About 1 hour

A perfect foil for spicy Mexican dishes is comfortingly mild yellow cornbread. If you like, add diced green chiles to give the bread extra punch.

- 2 eggs
- ¼ cup salad oil
- 1 small can (4 oz.) diced green chiles (optional)
- 1 small can (about 9 oz.) cream-style corn
- ½ cup sour cream
- 1 cup yellow cornmeal
- ½ teaspoon salt
- 2 teaspoons baking powder
- 2 cups (8 oz.) shredded sharp Cheddar cheese

In a large bowl, beat eggs and oil until well blended. If desired, add chiles; then mix in corn, sour cream, cornmeal, salt, baking powder, and 1½ cups of the cheese. Stir until well blended. Pour batter into a greased 8- or 9-inch baking pan and sprinkle with remaining ½ cup cheese.

Bake in a 350° oven until a wooden pick inserted in center comes out clean and crust is lightly browned (about 1 hour). Makes 6 to 8 servings.

Per serving: 311 calories, 11 g protein, 21 g carbohydrates, 21 g total fat, 105 mg cholesterol, 535 mg sodium

Pan Dulce

MEXICAN SWEET BUNS

Preparation time: About 50 minutes
Rising time: About 2¼ hours
Baking time: 15 to 17 minutes

Seashells, horns, and ears of corn—these are a few of the fanciful shapes that can be created from this classic sweet dough. Fill or top each bun with a generous dollop of buttery streusel.

- 6 tablespoons butter or margarine, cut into chunks
- 1 cup milk
- 1 package active dry yeast
- 1 teaspoon salt
- ⅓ cup sugar
  About 5 cups all-purpose flour
- 2 eggs
  Plain Streusel and Chocolate Streusel (recipes follow)
- 1 egg beaten with 2 tablespoons milk

In a small pan, combine butter and the 1 cup milk; heat over low heat to 110°F (butter need not melt completely). Meanwhile, in large bowl of an electric mixer, combine yeast, salt, sugar, and 2 cups of the flour. Pour in warmed milk mixture and beat, scraping often, on medium speed for 2 minutes. Blend in the 2 eggs and 1 more cup of the flour;

beat on high speed for 2 more minutes. With a spoon, gradually beat in enough of the remaining flour to form a stiff dough.

Knead dough on a floured board until smooth and elastic (about 5 minutes). Place in a greased bowl; turn to grease top. Cover and let rise in a warm place until doubled (about 1½ hours).

Meanwhile, prepare Plain Streusel and Chocolate Streusel.

Punch dough down and turn out onto a floured board. Divide into 14 equal pieces; shape each into a smooth ball. Shape 7 of the balls into seashells by patting dough into 3-inch rounds. Squeeze ¼ cup of either streusel into a firm ball; then press over top of each round. Score in a cross-hatch pattern or with slightly curved parallel lines to resemble a scallop shell.

Roll remaining dough into 4- by 8-inch ovals. Top each with 3 tablespoons of either streusel. To make horns, roll oval from short end; stop halfway, fold in sides, and finish rolling. Curl in ends to form a crescent. To make ears of corn, completely roll up ovals from short end. Slash tops crosswise with a knife, cutting halfway through dough.

Place buns about 2 inches apart on greased baking sheets. Cover lightly and let rise until doubled (about 45 minutes). Brush with egg mixture and bake in a 375° oven until lightly browned (15 to 17 minutes). Makes 14 buns.

Plain Streusel. Stir together ½ cup **sugar** and ⅔ cup **all-purpose flour**. With a pastry blender or your fingers, mix in 3½ tablespoons cold **butter** or margarine until fine crumbs form. With a fork, blend in 2 **egg yolks**.

Chocolate Streusel. Prepare **Plain Streusel** (above), stirring 2 tablespoons **unsweetened cocoa** or ground chocolate into flour mixture.

Per bun: 424 calories, 9 g protein, 64 g carbohydrates, 15 g total fat, 168 mg cholesterol, 294 mg sodium

Rosca de los Reyes
THREE KINGS BREAD

Preparation time: About 45 minutes
Rising time: About 2 hours
Baking time: 25 to 30 minutes

Mexicans celebrate Twelfth Night (January 6) with this traditional fruit-laced yeast bread. Baked in a ring and garnished with "jewels" of candied fruits and nuts, each loaf resembles a royal crown.

Customarily, a tiny ceramic doll or lima bean is hidden in the bread. The guest who receives the piece with the treasure is obliged to give another party on February 2, also a religious holiday.

2 packages active dry yeast
1 cup warm water (about 110°F)
   About 5¼ cups all-purpose flour
¼ cup instant nonfat dry milk
1 cup (½ lb.) butter or margarine, at room temperature
½ cup granulated sugar
1 teaspoon salt
3 eggs
½ cup *each* raisins and chopped walnuts
¼ cup chopped candied cherries
1 tablespoon *each* grated orange peel and lemon peel
3 tablespoons half-and-half
2 cups sifted powdered sugar
½ teaspoon vanilla
   Candied fruits and nuts for decoration

In a large bowl, stir yeast into warm water and let stand until softened (about 5 minutes). Add 1¼ cups of the flour and dry milk; beat well with a wooden spoon for 2 to 3 minutes. Cover and set aside in a warm place for 30 minutes.

Meanwhile, in another bowl, beat butter, granulated sugar, and salt until blended. Beat in eggs, one at a time. Add to yeast mixture and beat for 3 minutes. Gradually stir in enough of the remaining flour to make a stiff dough.

Knead on a well-floured board until dough is smooth and elastic (about 8 minutes). Place in a greased bowl; turn to grease top. Cover and let rise in a warm place until doubled (about 1½ hours).

Combine raisins, walnuts, cherries, orange peel, and lemon peel in a small bowl. Punch dough down and turn out onto a floured board; pat into a 10-inch round. Top dough with fruit-nut mixture, fold up edges, and knead until fruits and nuts are evenly distributed.

Divide dough in half; shape each half into a roll about 20 inches long and place each roll on a greased baking sheet. Join ends to form rings. Cover lightly and let rise in a warm place until puffy (about 30 minutes).

Bake, uncovered, in a 400° oven until bread sounds hollow when tapped on bottom (25 to 30 minutes). Let loaves cool on racks.

Stir together half-and-half, powdered sugar, and vanilla; drizzle evenly over loaves. Decorate with candied fruits and nuts. Makes 8 to 10 slices each (2 loaves).

Per slice: 316 calories, 6 g protein, 46 g carbohydrates, 13 g total fat, 67 mg cholesterol, 222 mg sodium

Celebrate with Latin flair by offering enchanting Polvorones de Nuez (recipe on facing page). They taste as exquisite with afternoon tea as with champagne. A coating of snowy powdered sugar makes these pastries irresistible. Because they keep well, they're an excellent holiday gift, too. Or just fill the cookie jar and indulge whenever you please!

Pan de Feria
CARNIVAL BREAD

Preparation time: About 40 minutes
Rising time: About 2 hours
Baking time: About 30 minutes

Inscribe "Happy Easter" or any other message on this slightly sweet bread, as bakers do at carnivals in Mexico. Practice your writing skills on wax paper; then scoop the mix back into the pastry bag to use.

- 1 **package active dry yeast**
- ¾ **cup warm water (about 110°F)**
- ½ **cup sugar**
- ½ **cup (¼ lb.) butter or margarine, at room temperture**
- 4 **eggs**
- ½ **teaspoon salt**
- 1 **teaspoon vanilla**
  About 4½ cups **all-purpose flour**
- 1 **egg beaten with 1 tablespoon water**
  Writing Mix (recipe follows)
  Sesame seeds and raisins (optional)

Stir yeast into warm water and let stand until softened (about 5 minutes).

In large bowl of an electric mixer, beat sugar and butter until blended; beat in the 4 eggs, one at a time. Mix in salt, vanilla, and yeast mixture.

Blend in 2 cups of the flour; beat at medium speed for 10 minutes. With a wooden spoon, stir in 2½ more cups of the flour until thoroughly moistened. Knead on a well-floured board until dough forms a smooth ball (2 to 3 minutes), adding more flour as needed. Place dough in a greased bowl; turn to grease top. Cover and let rise in a warm place until doubled (about 1½ hours).

Punch dough down and knead vigorously on a lightly floured board for 4 to 5 minutes. Shape into a smooth ball and place on a large greased baking sheet. Flatten ball and roll out into a 10- to 11-inch round. Cover loosely with plastic wrap and let rise in a warm place until puffy (about 30 minutes).

With a sharp knife, make a ⅛-inch-deep slash across center of loaf. Brush loaf all over with egg mixture.

Prepare Writing Mix. With a pastry bag fitted with a ¹⁄₁₆- to ¼-inch plain tip, use mix to write a message on loaf, avoiding area around slash. Reserve some of the mix. If desired, sprinkle loaf with sesame seeds and raisins.

Bake in a 350° oven until richly browned (about 30 minutes). Check loaf after 15 minutes; if decora-

tion has split, remove bread and fill in with reserved writing mix. Return to oven and finish baking.

Transfer to a wire rack and let cool for at least 10 minutes. Serve warm or at room temperature. Makes about 10 slices (1 large loaf).

Writing Mix. With a heavy spoon, mix ¼ cup **all-purpose flour** and ¼ cup **butter** or margarine, at room temperature, until smooth. Add 1½ teaspoons **water** and blend well.

Per slice: 420 calories, 10 g protein, 56 g carbohydrates, 17 g total fat, 174 mg cholesterol, 286 mg sodium

Polvorones de Nuez
MEXICAN WEDDING COOKIES

Pictured on facing page

Preparation time: About 40 minutes
Baking time: About 45 minutes

Mexico's delicate wedding cookies belong to a family of buttery confections, similar to shortbread, known as *polvorones*. These display a distinctive snowy coating of powdered sugar.

- 1½ **cups (¾ lb.) butter or margarine, at room temperature**
- ¾ **pound powdered sugar**
- 1 **egg yolk**
- 1 **teaspoon vanilla**
- ½ **cup finely chopped almonds**
- 3¼ **cups all-purpose flour**

Beat butter until light and fluffy; then beat in 2 tablespoons of the sugar, egg yolk, vanilla, and almonds. Gradually add flour, beating to blend thoroughly. Pinch off pieces of dough the size of large walnuts and roll between your palms into round balls. Place 1½ inches apart on ungreased baking sheets; flatten each ball slightly.

Bake in a 275° oven until very lightly browned (about 45 minutes). Let cool on baking sheets until lukewarm.

Sift half the remaining powdered sugar onto a large sheet of wax paper. Roll each cooky gently in sugar. With your fingers, pack more sugar all over cookies to a depth of about ⅛ inch. Place cookies on wire racks over wax paper and dust generously with more powdered sugar; let cool completely. If made ahead, store in airtight containers, layered between sheets of wax paper, for up to 3 days. Makes 3 dozen cookies.

Per cooky: 152 calories, 2 g protein, 17 g carbohydrates, 9 g total fat, 28 mg cholesterol, 79 mg sodium

Chocolate: Mexico's Gift to the World

An ancient Toltec legend recounts that the god Quetzalcoatl brought seeds for the cocoa tree down from heaven. Whether or not that actually happened, cocoa pods do provide a truly heavenly confection: chocolate.

And it was Mexico that introduced chocolate to the modern world in 1519 when the Aztecs let Cortés in on their secret. They served it to him in a cool, frothy drink, aromatic with spices and vanilla, but left unsweetened.

Today in Mexico, chocolate is still consumed mainly as a beverage—hot, sweet, and flavored with cinnamon and almonds. Tablets of chocolate, which have already been blended with sugar, cinnamon, and almonds, are used to prepare the drink. Easy to find beyond the Mexican border, these tablets, sold in Latin markets and many grocery stores, are packaged in brightly colored, octagonal boxes and labeled "Mexican chocolate." Use them to concoct traditional hot chocolate, orange-scented cake, and rich sauce for ice cream sundaes, following the recipes below (or substitute regular chocolate). Capture the same essences of Mexican chocolate in heavenly ice cream, made with cocoa, cinnamon, and almonds.

For an entirely different taste, try Mexico's unique way of using plain chocolate—the exquisite *mole poblano* sauce for poultry (page 76).

Mexican Hot Chocolate

Pictured on page 115

Froth this brew with a blender. Or whip it until foamy with the traditional Mexican chocolate beater, a *molinillo* (see photo), sold in Mexican stores and import shops. If Mexican chocolate is unavailable, Chocolate Almond Cocoa (recipe at right) is an easy substitute.

    1 quart milk
    1 tablet (3 oz.) Mexican chocolate, broken into
       wedges

To froth in a blender, warm milk in a 2-quart pan over medium heat until steamy; do not boil. Meanwhile, in a blender, finely chop chocolate. Pour in half the hot milk and whirl until blended; add remaining milk and whirl until very foamy.

To froth with a molinillo, combine milk and chocolate over medium heat and cook until chocolate is melted. Remove from heat and place knob end of molinillo in liquid. Twirl slender end vigorously between your palms; continue whipping until chocolate is very frothy. Makes 4 servings.

Per serving: 309 calories, 10 g protein, 29 g carbohydrates, 19 g total fat, 34 mg cholesterol, 121 mg sodium

Chocolate Almond Cocoa

Prepare in a blender as directed for **Mexican Hot Chocolate** (at left) but, instead of Mexican chocolate, use 3 ounces **semisweet chocolate** broken into pieces; 3 tablespoons **slivered almonds;** 1 tablespoon **sugar;** and 2 teaspoons **ground cinnamon.** Whirl together in blender. Add milk as directed.

Per serving: 309 calories, 10 g protein, 29 g carbohydrates, 19 g total fat, 34 mg cholesterol, 121 mg sodium

Mexican Chocolate-Orange Cake

Pictured on page 115

This rich, yet rustic, cake tastes best with a dollop of whipped cream atop each serving. Use either Mexican chocolate tablets or readily available semisweet chocolate. Orange peel and juice add a distinctive tang.

    1   cup blanched unsalted almonds
    2   tablets (3 oz. *each*) Mexican chocolate or
        6 ounces semisweet chocolate, chopped
    ¼   teaspoon ground cinnamon (1¼ teaspoons
        if using semisweet chocolate)
        Grated peel of 1 orange
        Pinch of salt
    5   eggs, separated
    ¾   cup sugar
    2   tablespoons fresh orange juice
        Pinch of cream of tartar
        About ½ cup powdered sugar
        Whipped cream

Line bottom of an 8-inch round baking pan with parchment paper, or grease and flour-dust bottom and sides of a pan. Set aside.

Spread almonds on a large baking sheet and toast in a 350° oven until lightly browned (about 7 minutes). Let cool completely. In a blender or food processor, combine nuts, chocolate, cinnamon, orange peel, and salt; whirl until finely ground. (Or mince nuts and chocolate as finely as possible by hand and mix with other ingredients.)

Beat egg yolks with sugar until thick and lemon colored; stir in orange juice and chocolate mixture. In a separate bowl, beat egg whites with cream of tartar until stiff peaks form. Stir a third of the egg whites into chocolate mixture; then fold in remaining egg whites.

Pour into prepared pan and bake in a 350° oven until cake starts to pull away from pan and center springs back when gently touched (about 45 minutes).

Let cool on a rack; then loosen from pan and invert onto a platter. Peel off parchment paper. Pat powdered sugar around sides of cake and serve with whipped cream. Makes 6 to 8 servings.

Per serving: 419 calories, 10 g protein, 48 g carbohydrates, 24 g total fat, 171 mg cholesterol, 63 mg sodium

Chocolate-Almond Ice Cream

Pictured on page 115

Ice cream (*helado*) is a passion in Mexico; this particularly dense and creamy version features the same cinnamon and almond flavors that accent Mexican chocolate.

⅔ **cup slivered almonds**
1 **tablespoon cinnamon**
2 **cups sugar**
¼ **cup all-purpose flour**
⅔ **cup unsweetened cocoa**
2 **eggs**
3 **cups half-and-half**
4 **cups whipping cream**
1 **tablespoon vanilla**

Spread almonds on a baking sheet and toast in a 350° oven until lightly browned (about 7 minutes). Set aside.

In a 2- to 3-quart pan, stir together cinnamon, sugar, flour, cocoa, eggs, and half-and-half. Cook over medium heat, stirring, until mixture comes to a gentle boil (about 12 minutes). Let mixture cool to lukewarm; then blend in whipping cream and vanilla. Cover; refrigerate for at least 2 hours or until next day.

Pour mixture into a 1-gallon ice cream freezer; freeze according to manufacturer's directions until partially frozen (dasher will be hard to turn). Add almonds and continue to freeze until dasher no longer turns.

If made ahead, cover and freeze for up to a month. Makes 10 to 12 servings (about 2 quarts).

Per serving: 522 calories, 7 g protein, 45 g carbohydrates, 37 g total fat, 156 mg cholesterol, 65 mg sodium

Mexican Chocolate Sundaes

For an irresistible blending of two cultures, enjoy an all-American banana split topped with a sauce made with Mexican chocolate. Or add cinnamon to regular semisweet chocolate sauce to give it the same Latin flavor.

2 **tablets (3 oz. *each*) Mexican chocolate, broken into wedges**
⅔ **cup whipping cream**
2 **or 3 small bananas**
Vanilla or coffee ice cream
Chopped toasted almonds

In a 1- to 2-quart pan, combine chocolate and whipping cream. Stir constantly over low heat until chocolate is melted (about 5 minutes). Set aside and keep warm.

Peel bananas and slice in half crosswise; then cut each piece in half lengthwise. Line 4 or 6 bowls with 2 banana slices each. Top with a scoop of ice cream and sprinkle with almonds. Pour chocolate sauce over each serving. Makes 4 or 6 servings.

Per serving of sauce: 291 calories, 3 g protein, 24 g carbohydrates, 23 g total fat, 30 mg cholesterol, 11 mg sodium

Cinnamon Chocolate Sundaes

Prepare as directed for **Mexican Chocolate Sundaes** (above) but, instead of Mexican chocolate, use 6 ounces **semisweet chocolate,** chopped, and ½ teaspoon **ground cinnamon** to make sauce. Makes 4 or 6 servings.

Per serving of sauce: 222 calories, 2 g protein, 17 g carbohydrates, 18 g total fat, 30 mg cholesterol, 10 mg sodium

Churros
FLUTED FRITTERS

Preparation time: About 30 minutes
Cooking time: About 45 minutes

Fluted spirals of tender, freshly fried dough are sold at street markets throughout Mexico. Dusted with either plain or anise-flavored sugar, the fritters are then enjoyed with coffee or hot chocolate.

- 1 cup water
- ¼ teaspoon salt
- 1 teaspoon granulated sugar
- ½ cup (¼ lb.) butter or margarine
- 1 cup all-purpose flour
- 4 eggs
- ¼ teaspoon lemon extract
  Salad oil
- ½ cup powdered sugar, sifted

In a 3- to 4-quart pan, combine water, salt, granulated sugar, and butter over low heat; cook, stirring, until butter is melted. Increase heat to high and bring mixture to a rolling boil. Add flour all at once and remove from heat; with a spoon, beat until mixture is smooth and thick and pulls away from side of pan. Add eggs, one at a time, beating well after each addition, until dough is smooth and shiny. Stir in lemon extract and let cool.

Pour oil to a depth of 1½ inches into a wide frying pan and heat to 375°F on a deep-frying thermometer. Meanwhile, spoon half the dough into a large pastry bag or cookie press fitted with a large star tip. Squeeze a 7- to 9-inch ribbon of dough into hot oil; slice off. Cook, 2 or 3 ribbons at a time, until well browned (about 5 minutes). With a slotted spoon, remove churros as cooked and drain on paper towels.

While still warm, sprinkle churros liberally with powdered sugar. Serve immediately. Makes about 1½ dozen churros.

Per churro: 182 calories, 2 g protein, 9 g carbohydrates, 15 g total fat, 75 mg cholesterol, 98 mg sodium

CHURROS WITH ANISE SUGAR

With a mortar and pestle or small grinder, pulverize 1 tablespoon **anise seeds**. Prepare **Churros** as directed above; add anise powder to powdered sugar and sprinkle over churros. Makes about 1½ dozen churros.

Per churro: 182 calories, 2 g protein, 9 g carbohydrates, 15 g total fat, 75 mg cholesterol, 98 mg sodium

Buñuelos
FRIED SWEET PASTRIES

Preparation time: About 1 hour
Cooking time: About 30 minutes

Lavishly dusted with cinnamon-sugar, these crisp, round pastries are an irresistible sweet treat. Fry them ahead, if you like; then reheat in the oven just before serving.

- 4 eggs
- 1¼ cups sugar
- 1 teaspoon *each* baking powder and salt
  About 2 cups all-purpose flour
  Salad oil
- 1 teaspoon ground cinnamon

In large bowl of an electric mixer, beat eggs and ¼ cup of the sugar until thick and lemon colored. Stir together baking powder, salt, and 1½ cups of the flour; gradually add to egg mixture, beating until well blended. Stir in ¼ cup more of the remaining flour.

Knead on a lightly floured board until dough is smooth and no longer sticky (about 5 minutes), adding more flour as needed.

Divide dough into 16 equal pieces. With floured hands, shape each piece into a ball. As balls are formed, cover with plastic wrap and let rest for 20 minutes. On a floured board, roll each ball into a 5-inch circle; stack circles, separating with wax paper.

Pour oil to a depth of 1½ inches into a wide frying pan and heat to 350°F on a deep-frying thermometer. Meanwhile, combine cinnamon and remaining 1 cup sugar in a round pan. When oil is hot, cook dough circles, one at a time, turning once, until golden brown (about 1½ minutes). As buñuelos are cooked, remove from oil, drain briefly, and coat with cinnamon-sugar. Sprinkle any remaining cinnamon-sugar over buñuelos. Serve warm.

If made ahead, let cool completely. Store airtight at room temperature for up to 3 days; freeze for longer storage, thawing unwrapped.

To recrisp, arrange buñuelos in double layers in shallow baking pans. Bake, uncovered, in a 350° oven until hot (6 to 8 minutes). Makes 16 buñuelos.

Per buñuelo: 198 calories, 3 g protein, 28 g carbohydrates, 8 g total fat, 69 mg cholesterol, 182 mg sodium

Satisfy your sweet tooth with an ancient confection: Mexican chocolate. Sample rich and creamy Chocolate-Almond Ice Cream and zesty Mexican Chocolate-Orange Cake. Or sip Mexican Hot Chocolate, scented with almonds and cinnamon and whipped to a froth with a wooden molinillo (recipes on pages 112 and 113).

Desserts & Beverages

Sweet and exotic, traditional Mexican desserts showcase indigenous flavorings. Vanilla, cinnamon, and citrus grace subtle custards and puddings, goat's milk lends tang to the popular *cajeta* (caramel sauce), and vibrant tropical fruits enrich ices and creams.

Mexico's variety of sweets is often credited to nuns, who created them for holidays or to honor visiting dignitaries. The recipes were an inspired blend of traditions from Spain and Mexico.

Just as refreshing any time of day are Mexico's special beverages. Choose from a rainbow of fruit purées, mixed with water, in a cooling *agua fresca*. Wine-based *sangria* quenches your thirst deliciously on a hot day, while warm and spicy hibiscus punch wards off winter's chill. For a fitting finish to any meal the year around, serve coffee Mexican-style, subtly fragrant with cinnamon.

Papaya Fresca con Lima
FRESH PAPAYA WITH LIME

Preparation time: About 10 minutes

As a snack on the beach, a light breakfast, or a juicy, luscious dessert, Mexicans adore fresh papaya. Arrange slices decoratively on a plate and serve with lime wedges.

   2 large ripe papayas
   1 lime, cut into 4 wedges

Peel papayas. With a sharp knife, cut fruit in half lengthwise; scoop out and discard seeds.

   Place papaya halves, peeled side up, on 4 dessert plates. Slice through fruit crosswise at ½-inch intervals. With flat of a knife, push down gently on back of fruit to fan out slices, or arrange in a pinwheel pattern. Offer with lime wedges to squeeze over each portion. Makes 4 servings.

Per serving: 79 calories, 1 g protein, 20 g carbohydrates, .29 g total fat, 0 mg cholesterol, 6 mg sodium

Nieve de Cherimoya
CHERIMOYA ICE

Preparation time: About 20 minutes
Freezing time: At least 3 hours (less if using ice cream maker)

Relative newcomers to North American produce markets, cherimoyas have a custardlike texture and rich, exotic flavor. From January to May, look for ripe cherimoyas that give when gently squeezed; or let underripe fruit mature at room temperature —don't refrigerate.

   1 large ripe cherimoya (about ¾ pound)
   ½ cup *each* sugar and water
   2 tablespoons orange juice
      Fresh mint sprigs

Cut cherimoya lengthwise into 8 wedges. Trim off and discard peel; scoop out seeds. Chop enough fruit to make about 1¼ cups.

   In a 1- to 2-quart pan, combine sugar and water. Bring to a boil over high heat; cook until mixture is reduced to ½ cup (about 5 minutes). Let cool completely.

   In a blender or food processor, combine cherimoya and orange juice; whirl until puréed. Mix in syrup.

   Pour mixture into a 9-inch square baking pan; cover and freeze until firm (about 1 hour). Break

fruit into small chunks. In a food processor or with an electric mixer, beat just until mixture forms a smooth slush. Wrap airtight and freeze until firm (at least 2 hours).

   Or freeze mixture in an ice cream freezer, following manufacturer's directions, until firm.

   If made ahead, freeze for up to 1 month. To serve, let stand at room temperature until slightly softened. Garnish individual servings with mint. Makes 4 servings.

Per serving: 152 calories, 1 g protein, 39 g carbohydrates, .22 g total fat, 0 mg cholesterol, .32 mg sodium

Jericalla
SPICED CUSTARD

Preparation time: About 20 minutes
Chilling time: At least 12 hours
Baking time: 25 to 30 minutes

Cinnamon's magic turns a simple baked custard into a south-of-the-border specialty known as *jericalla*.

   2 cups milk
   2 cinnamon sticks (*each* about 3 inches long)
   ½ cup sugar
   3 eggs, beaten

In a 1½- to 2-quart pan, combine milk, cinnamon, and sugar; bring to a gentle boil, stirring. Let cool slightly; cover and refrigerate for at least 8 hours or until next day.

   Heat milk mixture over medium-high heat to scalding. With a slotted spoon, lift out cinnamon sticks and set aside. Place eggs in a bowl and gradually beat in milk mixture. Pour into 4 custard cups or ramekins (at least ⅔-cup capacity each) and place cups in a baking pan.

   Place pan on middle rack of a 350° oven and add enough boiling water to come halfway up sides of custard cups. Bake, uncovered, until centers of custards jiggle only slightly when shaken gently (25 to 30 minutes). Remove custards from hot water; cover and refrigerate for at least 4 hours or until next day.

   If desired, rinse cinnamon sticks, break in half, and arrange one piece atop each custard cup. Makes 4 servings.

Per serving: 233 calories, 9 g protein, 32 g carbohydrates, 8 g total fat, 223 mg cholesterol, 112 mg sodium

Glistening with caramel and infused with fresh orange flavor, silken-textured
Flan de Naranja (recipe on facing page) presents the perfect conclusion to any Mexican
meal. To serve, cut this classic custard into wedges and garnish each with a sprig
of fresh mint. Offer tea, coffee, or sparkling wine as an accompaniment.

Flan

CARAMEL CUSTARD

Preparation time: About 20 minutes
Baking time: About 25 minutes
Chilling time: At least 6 hours

Mexico's most famous dessert is actually of Spanish origin. But today, the custard base is redolent with such native flavorings as cinnamon and vanilla.

- **4** **whole cloves**
- **2** *each* **whole allspice and cardamom pods, crushed**
- **1** **cinnamon stick (about 3 inches long), broken in half**
- **2** **cups milk**
- **1** **teaspoon vanilla**
- **1** **tablespoon cold water**
- **⅔** **cup sugar**
- **6** **eggs**

In a cheesecloth bag or tea ball, combine cloves, allspice, cardamom, and cinnamon. Place in a 2-quart pan with milk and vanilla; set aside.

In a small, heavy pan, mix water and ⅓ cup of the sugar. Stir gently until sugar dissolves. Place pan over high heat and cook syrup, swirling pan occasionally, until clear and medium-amber in color.

Immediately pour caramel into a 1½-quart soufflé dish or 9-inch pie pan; tilt and swirl dish to evenly coat bottom and halfway up sides. Set on a wire rack to cool (caramel will harden quickly).

Heat milk and spices over medium heat until steaming hot; remove from heat and let cool slightly. Discard spices. In a large bowl, beat eggs with remaining ⅓ cup sugar; gradually add milk, blending quickly with a wire whisk or fork. Pour egg mixture into prepared dish.

Place dish in a larger baking pan at least 2 inches deep. Place on middle rack of a 350° oven and add enough boiling water to larger pan to come halfway up sides of flan dish.

Bake, uncovered, until a very shallow crevice forms when center of custard is pushed with back of a spoon (about 25 minutes; about 15 minutes if using pie pan). Remove dish from hot water. Cover and refrigerate for at least 6 hours or until next day.

To unmold, loosen edge of flan with a knife; then cover dish with a rimmed plate. Invert quickly. (If necessary, briefly dip bottom of flan dish in hot water to loosen.) To serve, cut into wedges and top with caramel sauce. Makes 6 to 8 servings.

Per serving: 164 calories, 6 g protein, 20 g carbohydrates, 6 g total fat, 214 mg cholesterol, 82 mg sodium

Flan de Naranja

ORANGE FLAN

Pictured on facing page

Preparation time: About 20 minutes
Baking time: About 30 minutes
Chilling time: At least 6 hours

In tropical areas of Mexico, orange-garnished flan is often served as a smooth, sweet ending to meals.

- **2** **tablespoons cold water**
- **1** **cup sugar**
- **1** **cup orange juice**
- **2** **tablespoons lemon juice**
- **Grated peel of 1 orange**
- **6** **eggs**
- **Orange slices and fresh mint sprigs**

In a small, heavy pan, mix water and ¾ cup of the sugar. Stir gently until sugar dissolves. Place pan over high heat and cook syrup, swirling pan occasionally, until clear and medium-amber in color.

Immediately pour caramel into a 1½-quart soufflé dish or 9-inch pie pan; tilt and swirl dish to evenly coat bottom and halfway up sides. Set on a wire rack to cool (caramel will harden quickly).

Meanwhile, in a large bowl, combine remaining ¼ cup sugar, orange juice, lemon juice, orange peel, and eggs; beat until well blended. Pour egg mixture into prepared dish.

Place dish in a larger baking pan at least 2 inches deep. Place on middle rack of a 350° oven and add enough boiling water to larger pan to come halfway up sides of flan dish.

Bake, uncovered, until a knife inserted in center of flan comes out clean (about 30 minutes; about 20 minutes if using pie pan). Remove dish from hot water. Cover and refrigerate for at least 6 hours or until next day.

To unmold, loosen edge of flan with a knife; then cover dish with a rimmed plate. Invert quickly. (If necessary, briefly dip bottom of flan dish in hot water to loosen.) Garnish with orange slices and fresh mint. To serve, cut into wedges and top with caramel sauce. Makes 6 servings.

Per serving: 228 calories, 6 g protein, 39 g carbohydrates, 6 g total fat, 274 mg cholesterol, 71 mg sodium

Cajeta

MEXICAN CARAMEL

Preparation time: 5 minutes
Cooking time: About 20 minutes

Discover Mexico's popular sweet-tooth indulgence —*cajeta*, a thick, gooey caramel made with evaporated goat's milk. Enjoy it as a dip for fruit or cookies, or as a sauce with ice cream.

> 1 **can (12½ oz.) evaporated goat's milk**
> 1 **cup sugar**
> 2 **tablespoons butter or margarine**
>   **Dried fruit, cookies, or ice cream**

In a 3- to 4-quart pan, combine milk, sugar, and butter. Bring to a boil over high heat. Cook, stirring often, for 10 minutes. Continue to cook, stirring constantly (mixture scorches easily), until sauce darkens to a medium caramel color (about 10 more minutes). Thickened sauce should still flow from a spoon; it will thicken more as it cools.

If made ahead, cover airtight and refrigerate for up to 3 months. Serve in tiny bowls as a dip for fruit or cookies, or spoon over ice cream. Makes about 1 cup.

Per tablespoon: 92 calories, 2 g protein, 15 g carbohydrates, 3 g total fat, 9 mg cholesterol, 34 mg sodium

Capirotada

MEXICAN BREAD PUDDING

Preparation time: About 25 minutes
Baking time: About 35 minutes

For intriguing contrasts of flavor and texture, serve this pudding hot with vanilla ice cream.

> 1 **cup *each* firmly packed brown sugar and water**
> 1 **cinnamon stick (about 3 inches long)**
> ½ **loaf (1-lb. size) French bread**
> ½ **cup *each* toasted pine nuts, toasted slivered almonds, and chopped walnuts**
> 1 **cup raisins**
> ½ **pound jack cheese, cut into ½-inch cubes**
> 1 **tablespoon grated orange peel**
>   **Vanilla ice cream or whipped cream**

In a small pan, stir together sugar, water, and cinnamon; bring to a boil and cook until slightly thickened (about 5 minutes). Discard cinnamon.

Cut bread into ½-inch-thick slices. Toast slices; then break into large pieces. Place half the bread in a greased 9- by 13-inch baking dish. Top with half the pine nuts, almonds, walnuts, raisins, and cheese. Pour half the cinnamon syrup over all. Repeat layers and top with remaining syrup; sprinkle with orange peel.

Cover and bake in a 350° oven until hot in center (about 35 minutes; uncover during last 5 minutes). Serve warm, topping individual portions with ice cream. Makes 8 to 10 servings.

Per serving: 393 calories, 12 g protein, 49 g carbohydrates, 18 g total fat, 21 mg cholesterol, 263 mg sodium

Torta de Tortillas

SWEET TORTILLA STACK

Preparation time: About 15 minutes
Baking time: 25 to 30 minutes

Ever versatile, the tortilla turns out a delicious dessert when layered with sweetened cream cheese and sprinkled with cinnamon. Serve with coffee after dinner or as an afternoon treat with Mexican Hot Chocolate (page 112).

> 2 **packages (8 oz. *each*) cream cheese, at room temperature**
> 1 **teaspoon grated lemon peel**
> 1½ **tablespoons lemon juice**
> ⅔ **cup plus 1 tablespoon firmly packed brown sugar**
> 2 **teaspoons ground cinnamon**
> 10 **flour tortillas (7- to 9-inch diameter)**
> 1½ **tablespoons butter or margarine, melted**
> 4 **fresh or canned peaches, sliced (optional)**

Beat together cream cheese, lemon peel, lemon juice, ⅔ cup of the sugar, and 1 teaspoon of the cinnamon. Place a tortilla on an ungreased rimmed baking pan. Spread with about ⅓ cup of the cheese mixture and top with another tortilla. Repeat layers, ending with a tortilla on top. Brush with melted butter and lightly sprinkle with remaining 1 tablespoon sugar and 1 teaspoon cinnamon.

Bake, uncovered, in a 400° oven until lightly browned (25 to 30 minutes). Cut into wedges; if desired, offer with peaches. Makes 8 servings.

Per serving: 430 calories, 8 g protein, 50 g carbohydrates, 22 g total fat, 68 mg cholesterol, 457 mg sodium

Chongos Zamoranos

SWEET CHEESE PUDDING IN SYRUP

Preparation time: About 25 minutes
Standing time: About 1 hour
Cooking time: 6 hours

Dessert lovers traveling to Mexico should be sure to visit Zamora (southeast of Guadalajara), a town renowned for its sweet creations. *Chongos*—tender squares of cheeselike pudding floating in syrup—are one such specialty. Although cooking time is long, it involves only occasional glances at the pot.

Look for rennet tablets near the gelatin in supermarkets or health-food stores.

- 2 **quarts whole milk**
- 4 **rennet tablets, finely crushed**
- ¼ **cup cold water**
- 1¾ **cups sugar**
- 1 **tablespoon vanilla**
- 2 **cinnamon sticks (*each* about 3 inches long), broken into pieces**
- 2 **cups water or liquid from chongos**

In a 4- to 5-quart pan, heat milk over low heat to 110°F. Mix rennet with cold water, ¾ cup of the sugar, and vanilla; stir thoroughly into milk. Let stand at room temperature until set (about 1 hour). With a sharp knife, cut straight through mixture to bottom of pan to create a grid pattern of 1- to 2-inch squares.

Set pan over lowest heat and cook, uncovered, until chongos are white and tender-firm to touch (6 hours); *do not stir.* Check mixture occasionally to be sure it is not hot enough to cause motion in pan (this will break up chongos).

In a 3- to 4-quart pan, combine cinnamon, remaining 1 cup sugar, and water (or use chongos' liquid, carefully siphoned out of pan, pouring liquid through a paper-towel-lined sieve and adding enough water to make 2 cups). Bring mixture to a boil and cook, uncovered, for 5 minutes. With a slotted spoon, gently transfer chongos to hot syrup. Let stand until lukewarm; or chill before serving. If made ahead, cover and refrigerate for up to 2 weeks.

To serve, spoon several chongos and some syrup into individual bowls. Makes 6 servings.

Per serving: 433 calories, 11 g protein, 75 g carbohydrates, 11 g total fat, 46 mg cholesterol, 294 mg sodium

Crema de Mango

MANGO CREAM

Preparation time: About 15 minutes

Festive, yet simple, this parfaitlike dessert tastes pleasingly cool after a spicy meal. Ripe mangoes should be slightly soft, like ripe avocados.

- 5 **large ripe mangoes**
  Sugar
- 2 **oranges, peeled, seeded, and cut into small pieces**
- 1 **tablespoon lemon juice**
- 2 **cups whipping cream**
- ½ **cup chopped pecans**

Peel and pit mangoes. In a blender or food processor, whirl fruit until puréed. Transfer to a bowl and season to taste with sugar. Stir in oranges and lemon juice. Whip cream and fold into mango mixture. Pour into parfait glasses and sprinkle with pecans. Makes 10 to 12 servings.

Per serving: 228 calories, 2 g protein, 23 g carbohydrates, 16 g total fat, 44 mg cholesterol, 16 mg sodium

Piña al Horno

BAKED PINEAPPLE

Preparation time: About 10 minutes
Baking time: 20 minutes

End dinner on a fresh and festive note with sweetened, rum-laced baked pineapple.

- 1 **large pineapple (about 4½ lbs.)**
  Sugar
- 3 **tablespoons rum**
- ¼ **cup butter or margarine**

With pineapple on its side, cut off a thick, lengthwise slice (do not include green crown). With a grapefruit knife, remove fruit from both pieces of shell and cut into bite-size chunks; reserve deeper shell.

Sprinkle pineapple to taste with sugar and stir in rum. Mound in shell and dot with butter. Wrap completely (including crown) in foil. Bake in a 350° oven for 20 minutes. Serve warm. Makes 8 to 12 servings.

Per serving: 77 calories, .4 g protein, 11 g carbohydrates, 4 g total fat, 10 mg cholesterol, 40 mg sodium

Sangria

FRUITED WINE PUNCH

Pictured on facing page

Preparation time: About 10 minutes

Mexico's hot and spicy foods taste best when washed down with a truly refreshing drink. Long a favorite in Mexico, *sangria* has become popular on both sides of the border.

- 2 **cups fresh orange juice**
- ½ **cup orange-flavored liqueur**
- 1 **bottle (750 ml.) white zinfandel or rosé wine**
- ¼ **cup sugar**
- 1 **orange, thinly sliced**
  Ice (optional)

In a large pitcher or bowl, combine orange juice, orange liqueur, white zinfandel, and sugar. Stir to blend well; add orange slices. Refrigerate until chilled. Serve cold, over ice if desired, with an orange slice in each glass. Makes about 6 cups.

Per cup: 220 calories, 1 g protein, 28 g carbohydrates, .23 g total fat, 0 mg cholesterol, 8 mg sodium

Sangrita

TOMATO-ORANGE DRINK

Pictured on facing page

Preparation time: About 10 minutes

Served in Mexico as a chaser for tequila, tomato-base *sangrita* has a kick of its own. Offered straight in tall and cold glasses, it makes an eye-opening breakfast or afternoon bracer. Add green onions as swizzle sticks.

- 1 **cup tomato juice**
- 2 **cups fresh orange juice**
- ½ **cup lemon or lime juice**
- ¼ **teaspoon liquid hot pepper seasoning**
  Ice
- 4 **green onions (tops trimmed slightly)**

In a large pitcher, combine tomato juice, orange juice, lemon juice, and liquid hot pepper seasoning. Pour into ice-filled tumblers and add a green onion to each glass. Makes 4 servings.

Per serving: 76 calories, 2 g protein, 18 g carbohydrates, .4 g total fat, 0 mg cholesterol, 236 mg sodium

Agua Fresca

SUMMER FRUIT COOLERS

Pictured on facing page

Preparation time: About 20 minutes

Translated literally as "fresh water," colorful *agua fresca* mixes fruit pulp with water in a drink that's genuinely thirst-quenching rather than filling.

Try other summer fruits as well as those suggested below.

- 2⅔ **cups seeded, peeled, and coarsely chopped cantaloupe or watermelon**
- 3 **to 4 tablespoons sugar**
- 2 **to 3 tablespoons lime juice**
- 2 **cups water**
  Ice

In a blender, smoothly purée fruit; season to taste with sugar and lime juice. Combine fruit mixture and water in a large pitcher. If desired, pour through a strainer to eliminate pulp. Cover and refrigerate for up to a week. To serve, stir well and pour into tall glasses over ice. Makes about 1 quart.

Per cup: 75 calories, 1 g protein, 19 g carbohydrates, .3 g total fat, 0 mg cholesterol, 11 mg sodium

KIWI AGUA FRESCA

Prepare as directed for **Agua Fresca** (above), using 1⅔ cups peeled and coarsely chopped firm **kiwi fruit,** 2 to 3 tablespoons **sugar,** 2 teaspoons **lime juice,** and 2 cups **water.** Makes about 1 quart.

Per cup: 67 calories, 1 g protein, 17 g carbohydrates, .3 g total fat, 0 mg cholesterol, 4 mg sodium

STRAWBERRY AGUA FRESCA

Prepare as directed for **Agua Fresca** (above), using 2¼ cups rinsed and hulled **strawberries,** 3 to 4 tablespoons **sugar,** 1½ tablespoons **lime juice,** and 2½ cups **water.** Makes about 1 quart.

Per cup: 63 calories, 1 g protein, 16 g carbohydrates, .3 g total fat, 0 mg cholesterol, 2 mg sodium

To quench your thirst in Mexico, a parade of colorful beverages awaits you. Choose from (clockwise from lower left) a bracing Margarita; watermelon, cantaloupe, or kiwi Agua Fresca; scallion-swizzled Sangrita; garnet-hued Ponche de Jamaica; and fruity Sangria, with a floating orange slice. Recipes on facing page and page 124.

Margaritas

Pictured on page 123

Preparation time: About 10 minutes

One of Mexico's most popular exports is the refreshing tequila- and lime-based *margarita*, served in chilled glasses with tingling rims of salt.

    Coarse salt
¾ cup (6 oz.) *each* **tequila, triple sec, and fresh
    lime juice**
    About 1 cup crushed ice

Thoroughly chill 4 stemmed glasses (about ½-cup size). Invert glass rims briefly in cold water and then in coarse salt; set aside.

In a blender, combine tequila, triple sec, lime juice, and ice. Whirl until frothy and well blended. Serve immediately in salt-rimmed glasses. Makes 4 servings.

Per serving: 241 calories, .2 g protein, 18 g carbohydrates, 0 g total fat, 0 mg cholesterol, 738 mg sodium

Ponche de Jamaica
HIBISCUS-FLOWER PUNCH

Pictured on page 123

Preparation time: About 20 minutes
Cooking time: About 10 minutes
Steeping time: At least 8 hours

A New Year's tradition in Mexico, this richly hued hibiscus punch appears with cookies, breads, dried fruit, and nuts. Look for dried hibiscus flowers in Mexican markets near other packaged seasonings.

    7 **cups water**
    1½ **cups sugar**
    2 **ounces (about 2 cups) dried Jamaica (hibiscus)
       flowers**
    1 **bottle (750 ml.) rosé, well chilled**
    1 **bottle (32 oz.) club soda, well chilled**
       Ice
       **Thin slices of orange, lemon, and lime
       (optional)**

In a 4- to 5-quart pan, combine water, sugar, and flowers. Bring to a boil over high heat; stirring occasionally. Reduce heat and simmer, uncovered, for 5 minutes. Remove from heat and transfer to a nonmetal container. Cover and steep at room temperature for at least 8 hours or refrigerate for up to 4 days. Pour mixture through a wire strainer; discard flowers.

Pour into a large punch bowl; add rosé, club soda, and ice. If desired, float citrus slices on top. Makes 14 to 16 servings (about 3½ quarts).

Per serving: 106 calories, .1 g protein, 19 g carbohydrates, 0 g total fat, 0 mg cholesterol, 15 mg sodium

WARM JAMAICA PUNCH

Prepare as directed for **Ponche de Jamaica** (above), but add only wine, not club soda or ice, to flower mixture. Also add 2 **cinnamon sticks** (*each* about 3 inches long), ⅓ cup **rum,** and 2 tablespoons **lime juice.** In a large pan, warm punch over medium-high heat until hot. Pour into a large punch bowl and float **lime slices** on top. Makes about 3 quarts (12 servings).

Per cup: 157 calories, .2 g protein, 26 g carbohydrates, 0 g total fat, 0 mg cholesterol, 4 mg sodium

Ponche Rojo
SPICY RED WINE PUNCH

Preparation time: About 10 minutes
Cooking time: About 15 minutes

At a winter party, warmly welcome your guests with this sweet, fruit-enriched red wine punch.

    3½ **quarts water**
    3 **cups sugar**
    6 **cinnamon sticks (***each* about 3 inches long**)**
    3 **medium-size green or yellow apples, peeled,
       cored, and sliced ¼ inch thick**
    2 **tablespoons lemon juice**
    1 **cup *each* raisins and whole pitted prunes**
    2 **quarts (64 oz.) dry red wine**
    ¾ **cup rum**

In a 6- to 8-quart pan, combine water, sugar, and cinnamon. Bring to a boil over high heat and boil rapidly until reduced to 3 quarts (about 15 minutes). Discard cinnamon.

Meanwhile, mix apple slices with lemon juice. Add to hot syrup with raisins, prunes, red wine, and rum. Ladle into mugs, adding several raisins, a prune, and a few apple slices to each serving. Makes 12 to 16 servings.

Per serving: 320 calories, 1 g protein, 57 g carbohydrates, .2 g total fat, 0 mg cholesterol, 8 mg sodium

Ponche de Leche
MILK PUNCH

Preparation time: 5 minutes
Cooking time: 7 to 10 minutes
Chilling time: At least 12 hours

Similar in taste to *cajeta* (page 120), milk punch is thick, sweet, and delicious. Enjoy it plain or pour it over ice cream and drink like a milkshake.

- ⅓ cup sugar
- 1 quart milk, warmed
- 1 cinnamon stick (about 3 inches long)
  Vanilla ice cream (optional)

In a 4-quart pan, cook sugar over high heat, swirling pan occasionally, until deep amber in color (5 to 7 minutes). Pour in milk (mixture will foam vigorously). Reduce heat to medium, add cinnamon, and continue to cook, stirring constantly, until smooth (2 to 3 more minutes). Let cool; cover and refrigerate for at least 12 hours or until next day. Discard cinnamon.

To serve, pour into large cups or, if desired, place a scoop of ice cream in a large glass and fill with punch. Makes 4 to 6 servings.

Per serving: 143 calories, 5 g protein, 19 g carbohydrates, 5 g total fat, 23 mg cholesterol, 80 mg sodium

Rompope
MEXICAN EGGNOG

Preparation time: About 15 minutes
Cooking time: About 25 minutes
Chilling time: At least 2 hours

Rompope refers both to a bottled, egg-rich liqueur sold in Mexico and to a similar holiday beverage made at home with milk, eggs, sugar, and rum. It will remind you of light eggnog.

- 2 cups *each* milk and half-and-half
- ½ cup sugar
- 1¼ teaspoons vanilla
- 8 egg yolks
- ¼ to ½ cup light rum (optional)
- 4 to 6 cinnamon sticks (*each* about 3 inches long)

In a 3-quart pan, bring milk and half-and-half just to a boil over medium-high heat. Remove from heat and let cool; skim. Add sugar and vanilla.

Return to heat and bring to a boil (watch carefully to prevent bubbling over). Boil gently over medium heat for 20 minutes. Let cool; then skim.

In large bowl of an electric mixer, beat egg yolks at high speed until thick and lemon colored (about 5 minutes). Reduce speed to low and gradually add cooled milk mixture. If desired, stir in rum. Cover and refrigerate for at least 2 hours or until next day.

To serve, place a cinnamon stick in a glass and pour in eggnog. Makes 4 to 6 servings (about 1 quart).

Per serving: 305 calories, 9 g protein, 24 g carbohydrates, 19 g total fat, 404 mg cholesterol, 84 mg sodium

Café de Olla
MEXICAN COFFEE

Preparation time: About 15 minutes

Although traditionally brewed in an earthenware pot, or *olla*, this cinnamon-steeped beverage easily adapts to a drip-style coffee maker. For a stunning after-dinner drink, add a splash of liqueur and whipped cream. For details on *piloncillo*, see page 15.

- ½ cup ground coffee
- 1 cinnamon stick (about 3 inches long), broken in half
- 1 small (about 3 oz.) cone *piloncillo*, chopped, or 4 tablespoons firmly packed brown sugar (optional)
- 4 cups water

Place coffee in filter container of a drip-style pot; scatter cinnamon and piloncillo over coffee. Brew with water. Pour into cups. Makes 4 to 6 servings.

Per serving: 7 calories, .3 g protein, 2 g carbohydrates, 0 g total fat, 0 mg cholesterol, 6 mg sodium

MEXICAN AFTER-DINNER COFFEE

Prepare as directed for **Café de Olla** (above); or use plain coffee, sweetened if desired. For each serving, pour ½ to 1 ounce **coffee-flavored liqueur** into each cup or glass; add hot coffee and garnish with 2 tablespoons **whipped cream,** about 1 tablespoon grated **semisweet chocolate,** and 1 **cinnamon stick** (about 3 inches long).

Per serving: 148 calories, 1 g protein, 13 g carbohydrates, 8 g total fat, 17 mg cholesterol, 12 mg sodium

Index

Fluffy Sopaipillas (recipe on page 105) offer a warming snack on chilly days. The airy pillows of fried dough, drenched with honey, make a delightful breakfast pastry, too. It's customary to serve them with Mexican Hot Chocolate (recipe on page 112). One taste and you'll know why the tradition got started.